Selling is a Woman's Game

Selling is a Woman's Game

15 POWERFUL REASONS WHY WOMEN CAN OUTSELL MEN

Nicki Joy with Susan Kane-Benson

AVON BOOKS ◆ NEW YORK

SELLING IS A WOMAN'S GAME is an original publication of Avon Books. This work has never before appeared in book form.

AVON BOOKS
A division of
The Hearst Corporation
1350 Avenue of the Americas
New York, New York 10019

Copyright © 1994 by Nicki Joy with Susan Kane-Benson
Front cover art by Clifford Faust
Published by arrangement with the authors
Library of Congress Catalog Card Number: 94-6825
ISBN: 0-380-77416-X

Library of Congress Cataloging in Publication Data:

Joy, Nicki.
   Selling is a woman's game : 15 powerful reasons why women can outsell men / Nicki Joy with Susan Kane-Benson.
      p. cm.
   1. Selling. 2. Women sales personnel. I. Kane, Susan.
II. Title.
HF5438.25.J69   1994   94-6825
658.85'082—dc20   CIP

First Avon Books Trade Printing: December 1994

AVON TRADEMARK REG. U.S. PAT. OFF. AND IN OTHER COUNTRIES, MARCA REGISTRADA, HECHO EN U.S.A.

Printed in the U.S.A.

OPM   10 9 8 7 6 5 4

ACKNOWLEDGMENTS

□ □ □

Over the past twenty plus years Susan Kane-Benson and I have worked with and trained salespeople all over the country who have inspired the writing of this book. We have been grateful for the opportunity to share our knowledge with them and have also marveled at what they have taught us. Over the years we have also been privileged to be able to listen to the other great trainers out there, who have informed and enlightened us. During the multitude of seminars, programs, and courses that we have attended, we have taken volumes of notes. We will never stop learning about sales. We love the subject and hope that those of you whom we have bored at cocktail parties with the newest and best sales techniques or related stories will forgive us.

We also hope that the great trainers and teachers out there whose information we have used will forgive us as well. Our total involvement and evolvement in sales have created a situation that is a bit strange . . . as our information has come from so many sources that we often forget who said what . . . or if the idea was original or not. Though we have tried to give credit to all those who have contributed to the thoughts, techniques, and concepts behind this book, we are certain that we have forgotten someone along the way. Please understand that any omission in the credit area is only caused by our faltering memory.

In any event, the following is a list of some of the key people whose words and writings have helped us either in the sales aspect of this book or in the formulation of the concept behind it all: Aaron T. Beck, M.D., Jane Barr Stump, Ph.D., Tom Hopkins, Marilyn Loden, John Nesbitt, Tom Peters, Dave Stone, Deborah Tannen, Zig Ziglar. Additionally please see the listing of recommended readings and references.

We also want to express an appreciation to six special people for the part they played as we brought our concepts into book form: Audrey Adler Wolf, our agent, whose vision and ability opened the doors for us; Bob Mecoy at Avon Books, who believed in our message and enabled it to all happen; and Lisa Wager, who got us off on the right track with her clearly focused direction. Additionally, a heartfelt thanks to Beverly Pennacchinni for her advice and encouragement from the start. And to our editors, Tom Colgan and Jody Rein, whose guidance, enthusiasm, and inspiration were nothing less than magical.

CONTENTS

□ □ □

AUTHOR'S NOTE— DON'T MESS WITH MOTHER NATURE

□ □ □

Mother Nature blessed women with some very special gifts—the gift of gab, compassion, patience, emotion, endurance, tolerance, versatility, and resourcefulness, just to name a few. We are naturally good at telling stories, remembering birthdays, doing a thousand things at once, keeping track of where the family puts its belongings, chauffeuring, entertaining, listening, improvising, making it feel better, making it look better, making it go away, giving advice, encouraging decisions. And the list goes on. . .

Interestingly enough, it is these feminine traits that become effective and useful skills when transplanted into the professional arena. Promoting cooperation, maintaining pleasant relationships, building rapport, networking, interpreting what people mean, and detecting nuances are especially important commodities in the world of business today.

Now, I doubt that Mother Nature had a *sales career* in mind for us when she endowed us with these qualities. But I believe these skills, traits, characteristics, and tendencies are just the stuff that good salespeople are made of.

As a sales trainer and motivational speaker for high-ticket industries, I have spent literally thousands of hours working with sales professionals all across our country. While helping both men and women refine and perfect their selling skills, I couldn't help but notice that women took naturally to many of the more sophisticated sales techniques, and their persuasive expertise seemed instinctive.

Now, you may ask, are these traits innate or a result of socialization? I contend that it really doesn't matter at all. Do all women display these attributes? No, no pattern applies to everyone, but this does not lessen the validity and significance of the trend. It is important for the reader to understand that this book does not analyze or psychoanalyze women as a gender or diminish the effectiveness of men in the field of selling. It does, however, maintain that most women in sales have a distinct natural edge in fifteen crucial areas that can help them immeasurably to assist, motivate, persuade, and convince customers to buy what they are selling.

All readers will find this book an education in the subtleties of high-powered salesmanship. All women, I hope, will find this book to be a supreme confidence builder that heightens their awareness of their natural savvy and talents and empowers them to hone and use those skills with pride!

INTRODUCTION
SHE'S A NATURAL-BORN SALESMAN
□ □ □

Recently I realized that the last three major purchases I made were sold to me by women: my home, my computer, and at least two lifetime supplies of Mary Kay cosmetics. Obviously there are some women out there who know the answer to the question—Why sales? For those of you who do, this book will give you a deeper understanding of your profession and provide you with additional insight as to how to best use your natural sales talents to become even more of a superstar.

But for those of you who are wondering, Why Sales? I invite you to wake up and smell the cappuccino.

Sales is a wide-open field that has been notoriously dominated by men. Yes, men played the game well; after all, they made up the rules. In the past legitimate reasons existed for women to avoid the selling arena. The image of a salesperson was that of a fast-talking huckster. And let's face it, who would aspire to be that? It was an image that was "unladylike" and downright "unattractive." Sales required a pushy, coercive demeanor (which women were simply not supposed to display—at least not outside of their homes). Sales also required a plaid polyester suit (which most women would not be caught dead in).

Men reigned in the field of sales, and also controlled the world of business. That was their domain. They were the buyers and the sellers. They made the major purchase decisions for their companies and traditionally were comfortable working within the "all boy" network.

Sales required traveling. In fact, the phrase "traveling

salesman" became a cliché. And women traveling? Alone? Are you kidding? Straying from the home front was not only frowned upon for women (the family would starve, have no underwear, and forget to take baths), but it was also unsafe (there were killers out there, seductive strangers, and the car could break down).

Until the 1960s, the only form of sales that was acceptable for women was retail sales. This allowed women to be "protected." They worked behind the counter, in a store, with others, while customers came to them. The only aspects of salesmanship necessary were minimal product knowledge, an accommodating attitude, and a pleasant appearance. Of course, salaries reflected these very basic qualifications. Persuasion skills and sales techniques were generally not required.

Although retail sales has remained basically unchanged, salesmanship in general has undergone a dramatic conceptual metamorphosis. The rules have been changed and the masculine mold has been broken. Thankfully, overtly aggressive behavior and the hard sell are passé. Selling today has evolved into a fine-tuned craft that requires an understanding of the psychology of the buyer, skills in communication and leadership, and even responsiveness and sensitivity.

This change came about as consumers became more educated and less gullible, and were given more alternatives in terms of what to buy and who to buy it from. Today's consumers are smart, savvy, and sophisticated. It takes skill, not force, to sell to these people. Sales techniques have been redefined. These techniques must be practiced and smoothly executed—yet subtle—to win over the interest, attention, and loyalty of today's buyer.

The business world, too, has undergone a transformation. Although relatively few women sit on the boards of major corporations, since the early 1970s the number of women in middle management has doubled, rising to nearly 40 percent. Yes, the "all boy" network has been infiltrated, and men are, as a result, becoming more and more comfortable dealing with women in all phases of business, including sales.

In fact, female salespeople now make up over 51 percent

of the total sales force in the communications industry, over 39 percent in the printing and publishing business, over 35 percent in the electronics and instruments field, over 34 percent in office equipment sales, and over 64 percent in full-time real estate sales. Women are making inroads into every sales arena. Yes, today "she sells seashells" and much, much more.

Travel as part of a sales job may still seem like a real issue for many women today—but it is not. Computers, affordable long-distance phone systems, fax machines, Express Mail, convenient airline schedules, and the like have minimized the need for extensive travel. Even if travel is required, it can be accomplished expeditiously, more safely, and comfortably. And to top that off, according to a survey conducted for Residence Inn by Marriott, women fare far better on business trips than men. Specifically, they cope better with the frustrations of traveling, feel less lonely, demonstrate less boredom, and in many cases actually find it a treat to leave the home chores behind.

Still, there are many women out there who have never considered sales simply because they believe that selling is the process of making people buy something that they don't need. Selling is not that at all.

- **Selling is *helping* people discover *if* they need what you are selling.**

Selling does not require high pressure or force. Selling is not that at all.

- **Selling is *helping* people to buy something that they might not have bought without your assistance.**

Selling does not require an aggressive, pushy demeanor. Selling is not that at all.

- **Selling is *convincing* people of the value of your product and *persuading* them to see how it will enhance their lives.**

And come on, we as women, have been helping, convincing, and persuading for years. We *helped* our kids get well by getting them to swallow that terrible-tasting cough syrup. We *persuaded* the state trooper to give us a verbal warning instead of a written ticket. We *convinced* our mothers to let us wear eye shadow and lipstick in seventh grade.

So if you are first entering the sales arena, the key is to find a product that you believe in, understand the new skills involved in selling today, and see how these skills parallel what you already have as a woman. You will quickly see that it is *she*, not *he*, who is the "Natural-Born Salesman."

Good news, too! A sales career doesn't have to be preceded by a formal education, and experience is not a necessity. That's right, you read it here, experience is not a necessity. In fact, more and more companies are actually attracted to people with less sales experience. They are finding it easier to train someone in their own image with the new sales techniques than to retrain someone with an outdated sales approach that might not coincide with company philosophy or current consumer needs.

Why else sales? Hours can be flexible, your home can often be your office, and the bucks are good! So selling ain't what it used to be! The changes beckon women—especially with our innate ability to *help, persuade, and convince*.

As Eleanor Emmons Maccoby and Carol Nagy Jacklin state in their book, *The Psychology of Sex Differences:*

> *What about the male pattern of aggression and dominance attempts—are there occupations to which these contribute positively? Undoubtedly there are some, although it is difficult to know precisely what they are. It was once thought that a salesman needed to be "aggressive," but it is now known that a softer approach can be equally or sometimes more effective. A salesman does need to convey a sense of confidence in himself and his product, but the ability to do this is by no means a special province of the male.*

If you need more proof that you, as a woman, have a gift for sales, I have developed a short quiz to help you see if you have the attributes that lead to sales success. We encourage every woman reading this to linger on this page a moment and take this quiz. We know that you as women don't need much encouragement to do this. Women love quizzes. They love to take them and to give them. Women's magazines are loaded with quizzes. Men, on the other hand, don't like quizzes. They don't want to take them or give them. Men's magazines don't have quizzes in them. (In fact, many men's magazines don't even have words in them).

A QUIZ THAT COULD CHANGE YOUR LIFE

1. Do you find that you do many more things at once than most of the men you know?   **Yes No**

2. Do you feel that you take more time with your appearance than the men you know?   **Yes No**

3. Do you find that though men may make the big plans, it is you who has to take care of all the details?   **Yes No**

4. Do you find that when meeting someone new, you are more interested than your male partner in finding out what you two have in common?   **Yes No**

5. Do you tend to flatter and praise others more than the men you know?   **Yes No**

6. Do you ask more questions in conversation than the men you know?   **Yes No**

7. Do you think that you listen to what others have to say better than men?   **Yes No**

8. Do you feel that when trying to convince someone to do something, you will take more time to explain "why" than the men you know?   **Yes No**

9. Do you seem to have more of an interest in communicating than the men in your life have?   **Yes No**

10. Do you like to make "connections" with people and welcome involvement? **Yes No**

11. Do you thrive on harmony and agreement rather than controversy and discord? **Yes No**

12. Do you feel that you are intuitive? **Yes No**

13. Do you make more "to do" lists than the men you know? **Yes No**

14. After an event, do you like to recap what happened, either to yourself or with a friend? **Yes No**

15. Do you make more of an effort to keep in touch with others than the men in your life? **Yes No**

If you answered "yes" to thirteen out of the fifteen questions . . . get ready, a new money-making career may be right around the corner. Read on to learn why these fifteen feminine attributes can enable women to outsell men without even trying.

Selling is a Woman's Game

– 1 –
ALL SUPERHEROES WEAR PANTY HOSE

□ □ □

REASON #1
Women Are Happy Jugglers

Sales requires engaging in a multitude of tasks simultaneously, playing many varying roles concurrently, and having the strength, stamina, and ability to keep an eye on it all. These skills, shared by superheroes and women, can launch you on a superstar sales career.

Spiderman, Superman, Marine Boy, Batman, and Robin all have one thing in common . . . panty hose. It seems that all superheroes wear panty hose. It's no surprise, then, that many women of today are called Superwomen and that we can become "Super-*Sales*women" in a snap . . . but it's not just because of that panty hose connection. The Superwoman designation came about because of our ability to do it all:

USE TIME PRODUCTIVELY
DISTRIBUTE ENERGIES EASILY
ENGAGE IN A MULTITUDE OF TASKS EFFORTLESSLY
KEEP A PULSE ON IT ALL EFFECTIVELY

These talents make us seem invincible and unstoppable in life—and these talents are critical prerequisites in the field of sales. Yes, women already have what it takes. Just watch any woman during the course of her day to see these superpowers in action.

1

The other day I was having a meeting with a female executive who was responsible for selling millions of dollars worth of real estate. Within two minutes, Beverly escorted me into her office, offered me a seat, handed me a cup of coffee, and produced a market study that was turned to the exact page we needed to review. The phone rang. Before even having a chance to say more than a quick hello to this caller, her second line rang and she smoothly transitioned, putting caller number one on hold. She apologized to me and picked up line number two. For the next several minutes the conversation I overheard went something like this:

BEVERLY TO CALLER #2:	"Is that pile of wood warped on lot 221? I'll hold; check with Frank."
BEVERLY TO CALLER #1:	"Take the macaroni and cheese casserole out of the freezer. It is behind the frozen waffles. Do that and I'll wait."
BEVERLY TO ME:	"Research indicates that a conversion rate of 5 percent is an absolute necessity on that job."
BEVERLY TO CALLER #2:	"Well, it looked warped to me. Did the shipment of header boards and joists come in? Ask Doris. I'll hold."
BEVERLY TO CALLER #1:	'*No!* You can't put metal in a microwave. Take off the aluminum foil and cover it with some Saran Wrap."
BEVERLY TO ME:	"In other words, the plan involves using unconventional marketing methods to generate traffic. You mentioned that there are over eleven thousand special-interest magazines in the country today. Do you think we should go that route?"
BEVERLY TO CALLER #2:	"Great! I'll be out later this afternoon with the new spec sheets and punch list."

BEVERLY TO CALLER #1: "OK, now set the timer on high for twelve minutes. Forget the tossed salad if it is too much trouble, and why don't you just try putting the baby in the swing for a while."

Talk about using time productively, distributing energies easily, engaging in many tasks effortlessly, and keeping a pulse on it all. Now, one may surmise that these abilities evolved in women out of necessity, considering the variety of tasks involved in keeping the home fires burning. There may indeed be some truth to that. But these abilities became even more finely tuned as more and more of us entered into the work arena. Let's face it, many women who work outside the home face a full evening of work once they get home.

Research, in fact, supports our dual full-time jobs, and some statistics offered by experts in the field are rather astounding. Muriel Fox, a nationally known spokeswoman on women's issues, says that a wife who also works outside the home does as much as twenty hours of work in the home, while men who work outside the home engage in only about thirty minutes of housework per week.

Even though times are a-changin' and men's involvement in the daily chores of running the home has increased dramatically, the inequities in the work and responsibility load are still, in most cases, frustratingly blatant. In fact, even when men take on some of the household tasks, they rarely keep a pulse on the whole picture and seem to have difficulty taking on more than one task at a time.

For example, many of the men I know have voiced high anxiety when given the job of meal preparation. A common complaint centers around getting the timing down. In other words, getting the peas, meat loaf, and baked potato ready at the same time for the same meal, on the same day. Sure, men can learn with practice—there are plenty of great male chefs—but add in a crying baby, the kid who needs to be picked up from soccer practice, watering the plants, making the congratulations call, paying the newspaper boy, and putting in the fabric softener . . . and you need a woman to do the job!

The ability that women have to be multifocused began to develop in most cases at an early age. Girls watched and often helped as their mothers engaged in many chores at once. In preparing for their own futures, they accepted the fact that doing many things well, at the same time, was a required and essential part of a woman's role.

Yes, women's apparent ease in successfully managing a multitude of diverse tasks simultaneously stems in part from socialization. Women have developed, as a function of the demands of their roles in society, an alertness, and sensitivity to their surroundings. That alertness and sensitivity contribute heavily toward enabling women to keep a pulse on many things at once, to make connections, to observe changes in the environment, to deal with the less concrete, and to anticipate . . . to see ahead and to think ahead.

Studies have shown that men tend to compartmentalize their lives more than women. Their tendency to focus on only one thing at a time is well known. (A popular comedienne, Rita Rudner, commented that she gets consistently frustrated when taking a ride with her boyfriend. She states that he is so focused that when he gets lost, he has to turn off the car radio, and take the gum out of his mouth, to think about what the proper next turn should be.)

Women, on the other hand, operate quite differently. Janet Kolesar, associate professor of biology at Ursuline, states, "Women can see the forest as well as the trees."

Additionally, perhaps men avoid these multiagenda situations because of the stress they cause. Women, according to scientific research, have more built-in hormonal protection that enables them to better tolerate and cope with chronic stress than men. As Dr. Estelle Ramey of Georgetown Medical School states, "Physiologically, women don't cave in to stress as easily as men, and that is why they live longer."

The configuration of the female brain may be another factor accounting for women's ability to handle diverse tasks. The fiber connections between the right and left sides of a woman's brain are significantly more numerous that those in a man's. That factor seems to better enable women to effectively handle several problems or tasks at once with little difficulty.

Yes, because of a hormonal structure that enables one to better cope with stressful situations, a brain that can quickly transfer information back and forth between the emotional and rational hemispheres, and socialization that encourages developing multitask ability, women are easily able to juggle at home and on the job.

Additionally, research proves that we are happy jugglers. Although, obviously, handling a variety of roles with a minimum of support can be frustrating and stressful, when some support exists, women actually thrive and are happier in multirole situations. According to Dr. Lois Verbrugge of the University of Michigan in her paper on "Women's Social Roles and Health," the multiple roles that women engage in seem to have a positive enhancing effect on their attitude toward life. So juggling may be better for us than we would first think.

Have you ever seen those really advanced jugglers, performers who can juggle all sorts of different things? They can keep a banana, a chair, a stick of gum, a bowling ball, and a flaming sword all going at the same time with incredible ease. I equate that type of juggling (juggling things of different natures) with what is required in the business of sales. And since we as women are already good at juggling, and enjoy it, with a little more insight we will be well on our way to becoming the advanced jugglers who make sales superheroes.

You see, being successful in sales will require juggling not only many different people, but many different people in many different aspects of the sales process. A sale normally consists of a series of steps, and chances are you won't be at the same step with every customer at the same time.

So let's now take a look at the steps involved in most sales. Each step, once successfully completed, will enable you to move on to the next. Those of you who are already experienced in sales will understand my breakdown of the process and probably follow these same steps every day.

UNDERSTANDING AND PERFECTING
THE SALES PROCESS

Throughout this book, I will be delving further into each of these concepts to help you perfect the sales process. But more important, I will encourage you to understand and use your natural abilities to execute the elements of the sale. First, however, you must understand the basic elements of that process.

- **Preparation**—Product knowledge is critical to help you understand your product's worth and value as well as to fortify your self-confidence and to project credibility. This involves knowing your product up and down—inside and out. It also involves knowing the competition just as well.

- **Prospecting**—It is foolish to think that even under the best of situations (such as entering a company with a lead list a mile long), you can rely totally on your company for customers. All good salespeople develop a proficiency in prospecting. This involves networking, nurturing referrals, keeping up with past clients, following up on the lead, and finding creative ways to broaden your prospect base.

- **Creating a relationship**—Making yourself the kind of person whom customers want to deal with involves having more than product knowledge. It involves conveying the right personal image, having the ability to build rapport and trust, and using the communication and people skills necessary to create a bond.

- **Assessing your buyer and uncovering needs**—Trying to sell to someone who has no need at all for your product will prove frustrating at the very least. This is not to say that all people *recognize* their needs, or that you can't help them *uncover* their needs; i.e., to see the value of buying what you are selling. However, since we sell to the people we know most about, learning about your buyers—determining their buying qualifications, matching opportunities (discovering what they need that you have), and assessing their interest level and feelings—will enable you to sell to the people who can buy. This requires a superior ability to ask, listen, and read beyond the words.

- **Demonstrating**—Creating buyer involvement with your product is essential. It makes people *want* what you are selling. They may need it, they may be able to afford it, but unless they want it, they won't buy it. Demonstrating your product gives you the best opportunity to create the involvement that strongly connects the buyer with what you are selling.

- **Handling objections**—Consumer objections are a very real part of the buying process. Nine times out of ten, the raising of an objection actually demonstrates interest in what you are selling. Therefore, objections should be music to a salesperson's ears, as involved people raise objections. The key in selling is to know how to handle buyer resistance.

- **Closing**—Closing is making the sale. Closing is a learned skill. You reach the closing point only by properly executing the other steps along the way. Then it takes your ability to sum it all up, tie it all together, create the "buy now" reason, and actually *ask* for the order.

- **Follow through**—Since many sales are not accomplished the first time out, assuring another selling opportunity is critical. Follow-through involves not only the act of reconnecting with the prospect, but it demands knowing how to prime, prepare, and program the prospect for another encounter with you.

Next, you must develop a time management system to be effective, not just efficient.

AN APPROACH TO MANAGING YOUR TIME

Most people don't really manage their time; their time manages them. In other words, we operate on a panic basis. We do it when it becomes a panic or a "must do" situation. That was certainly the case with me.

What really shook me the most, when I started to study the subject of time management, was acknowledging the fact that time is an equal opportunity employer, so to speak. Each person on the face of the earth has exactly the same number of hours and minutes every day to work with, and some people just managed to do more with their 86,400 seconds every day than I did.

Then I made a discovery. Success and happiness in life depend on using your time effectively on a day-to-day basis. This requires: (1) keeping a tempo that allows you to be able to do all that you need to do (that tempo, I refer to as rhythm); (2) staying surefooted by keeping perspective and understanding what is important at the time (that surefootedness, I refer to as balance).

Though women have superior juggling skills, they must check themselves daily to make certain that their rhythm is comfortable and that they are in balance. Certainly there will be days that are more hectic and demanding than others, but if you keep aware of your rhythm and balance, they won't get out of hand and lifestyle patterns won't develop that make you feel out of control. Be aware of:

- **Exhaustion:** Some women have difficulty managing their time well because they are simply exhausted. They haven't balanced their life with enough rest and sleep. Their perspective is off.

- **Passivity:** Other women have difficulty managing their time well because they are too passive. They let everything control them. They are more reactive than proactive. They haven't balanced their lives with enough drive and assertiveness.

- **Oversaturation:** Still other women have difficulty managing their time well because they are totally overwhelmed. They put too much on their daily agenda and, as a result, can't accomplish anything. They're juggling way too many balls.

- **Inflexibility:** There are those who have difficulty managing their time well because they are overorganized. They are too inflexible. They are obsessed with details and their rhythm doesn't allow them to let go at times.

- **Perfectionism:** Some women have difficulty managing their time well because they set unrealistic expectations for themselves. They have to always be A+ perfect. Stellar.

Yes, the essence that encompasses everything in this advanced juggling game is balance and rhythm. And for better balance and a smoother rhythm, you have to understand some critical concepts about time management.

THE KEYS TO MANAGING YOUR TIME

1. It is only possible to live happily one day at a time. I'm not saying that you shouldn't plan for tomorrow, but consistently looking ahead and ignoring today can prove frustrating, disheartening, and disappointing.

2. Every single day must be planned for. Some of the plans might be made in advance and some may be made on the very day. Try to plan everything (within reason), even if it involves planning to do nothing for a portion or all of that day. A plan is a necessity, but keeping to it is not. Remember it is OK to change the plan.

3. Plan for rest, recreation, and relaxation. Some people are obsessed with being productive. They have a sense of guilt about being nonproductive and they always have to be doing something useful. (I could never watch TV without folding underwear.) They don't understand that reading a magazine and having a cup of coffee can be productive, that taking a walk in the park or playing checkers with the kids can be productive.

Effective time management requires that you understand that rest, recreation, and relaxation are essential parts of the regenerative rhythm, the productive rhythm that we all need. It is just not productive or wise to run any machine until it overheats and breaks down; that goes for your body and mind as well.

4.   Commit yourself to making quicker decisions. Decisiveness is a universal quality of all great leaders. Now, those decisions may not always be the right decisions, but making them quickly allows the rhythm to keep moving. One way you can accomplish this goal is by making a commitment not to "ponder the petty" or "drown in the drivel." In other words, keep things in perspective. How critical is this decision? Is it really worth spending time on? All decisions do not deserve equal time.

5.   Understand what simple cycles of activity are and how they make up our day. Each cycle of activity is made up of basically three steps: "commence, continue, conclude." Have you noticed that we are the happiest when we can scratch off or cross out a completed cycle of activity from our list? I have a friend who understands the importance of patting herself on the back or making a big deal out of completing a cycle of activity. Next to each crossed-out item on her daily agenda she writes the word "Victory."

6.   Make the commitment. Managing time wisely involves a commitment to do one thing every single evening. That one thing is to sit down and make up a list of priorities for the next day and number them in order of importance. If you don't do that, you are going to find yourself running around dashing from here to there, grabbing the next thing that happens to catch your attention. You will keep so busy that you will overlook things that you really want to do. Though the multitude of books on time management differ in approach, this is one step that they all seem to agree on.

When you take the time each night to write your "to do" list down in order of importance, a very interesting thing occurs. Your subconscious mind will take over and help you work on this list all night long. With your subconscious given direction and busily engaged in something productive, believe it or not, you will get a better night's sleep. Without the list, your subconscious is in a panic mode, thinking, "I have to remember to do this, I have to remember to do that."

The subconscious really does want to help you solve your problems and achieve your goals, but it can't help unless you take the time to tune it in and turn it on to what is going to happen next. When you list out the things you have to do, you ignite the power of your subconscious mind, and upon waking in the morning, you'll often find that fresh and creative problem-solving ideas will have surfaced.

So discipline yourself to make that list. Don't dwell on it. Be alone when you do it and feel positive that you can achieve your objectives. That positive attitude is critical for your subconscious to work *for* you. You see, *your* mind is *your* mind, and if you really don't feel you can do what you set out to do, or if you really don't want to accomplish it, you can bet that your subconscious mind will find a way to help you come up with an excuse to procrastinate or a means to fail. In other words, if you think you can do it, you are right, and if you think you can't . . . you'll be right, too.

7. Organize your time and daily life using *one* calendar. One item that has helped me immeasurably in organizing my time and daily life is my calendar, my one calendar, my one simple calendar. Since we have multiple roles, the temptation is to have a calendar for each role. It rarely works. Have one calendar, keep it with you always, but make sure it has room on it so that each week you have space to make the following lists:

- What to buy
- Whom to call
- Whom to write
- Things to think about
- Things to remember

Places to go and appointments should be recorded in the space allotted for each individual day. The lists should be checked three times a day and activities firmly crossed off when complete. This gives you an opportunity to see a cycle of activity happen, and remember, most of us get a great deal of pleasure from completing a cycle.

Personally, I find the hundred-dollar organizers out there,

with multicolored tabs, graph paper, maps of major cities, time zones, centigrade to Fahrenheit conversions, etc., to be a lot to do about nothing. Instead of organizing one's life, I think they tend to complicate it. My God, it takes me a half hour just to figure out whether to write the note down in the "tasks to complete," "information to process," or "pending programs" section.

On the other hand, beware of the sticky note pad syndrome. I went through this phase. I was a sticky note pad fanatic. I had notes all over the place, and I have to admit that even when I purchased my first organizer, it was not too long until the leather cover was festooned with sticky notes.

Experts say that it takes eleven to twenty-one days for a habit to take hold. I highly recommend that you try to discipline yourself for one month (if you're like me, you'll need the extra time) to use this one-calendar system. Warning: If you lose this calendar, you are dead. I therefore also recommend photocopying your updated calendar each week. I keep this copy in a vault.

Women, take heart. Although organizing yourself to be effective might not sound easy, Dr. Lynn Offerman, of George Washington University, conducted a management study that stated, "Women use time management techniques, such as keeping a daily log of jobs to be done, organizing jobs by priority, and scheduling important jobs for times of peak energy, more consistently than do men."

Since women have what it takes to get organized, use some of the methods and tips I've given you in this chapter to perfect your juggling skills, get your life in order, and ready yourself for the time of your life in the field of sales. There is no excuse for wasting another minute. It has often been said that "Time waits for no man," but they never said anything about an organized woman.

2

TRUST ME ON THIS ONE

□ □ □

REASON #2
It's Women Who Know How to Bond

We trust people who are most like ourselves and we trust people with whom we can agree. Women naturally build rapport with others by finding and creating similarities and seeking agreement.

I n our cynical world today there are more people than ever who enter a room, smell roses, and search for a coffin. Yes, people today think the worst, they are suspicious and skeptical. Can you blame them? After all, over the past several years, we have been bombarded with stories and exposés of religious leaders, politicians, bankers, physicians, and stockbrokers, to name a few, who have cheated, lied, and disillusioned us. How much can we take without turning sour? In fact, corruption, dishonesty, and deceitfulness have become so commonplace that they have almost lost their stigmas.

What does this mean to people in sales today? Unfortunately, stating that you have strong personal morals and pure business ethics is simply not enough to counter consumers' natural mistrust. Today you must know how to establish your credibility with clients, and you must know how to do it quickly, or they will go elsewhere. It means that to override the rising tide of cynicism and skepticism, **it is now more crucial than ever to understand and master the methods by which you can attain client trust.**

In sales, consumer/salesperson trust is *always* a factor. Establishing trust is a prerequisite for client loyalty and a continued business association. However, recognize that there is a positive correlation between the price of what is being sold and the trust factor the customer must feel toward the salesperson. In other words, the higher the ticket price of an item, the greater consumer trust must be.

No matter what you are selling, knowing how to establish trust with your client will give you the competitive edge. But if you are in high-ticket sales, establishing trust with your client is an absolute essential. Though we will explore two principles that encourage and foster trust, it must be remembered that in the final analysis it takes honesty, integrity, and reliability to really establish and maintain that trust.

There are two psychological principles related to creating trust that you should always keep in mind:

1. **We tend to trust people who are most like ourselves**
2. **We tend to trust people with whom we can agree**

Let's take a closer look at each principle.

WE TEND TO TRUST PEOPLE WHO ARE MOST LIKE OURSELVES

We can't help it, we just do. A few years back I was traveling in Greece and found myself in a section of Athens called the Plaka. The Plaka is the old square. Naturally there was an aura of mystery to it all, not just because this section of town is ancient, but because it was unfamiliar to me. I was having an adventure, but I was anxious. Everything was new and different.

There I was wandering around the Plaka, buying junk jewelry and drinking ouzo. Though the ouzo helped take the edge off this experience, I still found myself groping for something familiar.

All of a sudden, out of the crowd, I heard a man speaking English. It was amazing how quickly I found him. Approaching him, I said, "Excuse me, sir, but I heard you speaking English. Where are you from?" He responded, "The United

States." I cried out, "You're kidding. Me too!" (Big deal, right?) I probed a bit further, asking where exactly he was from in the United States. When he told me he lived in metropolitan Washington, D.C., specifically Maryland, I nearly keeled over. I was ecstatic. I jumped up and threw my arms around this man, yelling, "Me too, me too!" I found myself instantly trusting him and feeling that he was a real ally.

In retrospect, I realize this man could have been an escaped killer from a Maryland penal institution hiding out in Greece. However, I trusted him simply because we had an obvious commonality, a thread of harmony, a connection between us, a link: Maryland. In some way I found that we were *like each other*. This link, or likeness, worked very well to establish trust, especially in this unfamiliar and potentially uncomfortable environment.

Smart salespeople establish a common denominator base with their prospects, using this strategy to:

- Establish a feeling of similarity or likeness
- Increase the comfort level
- Diminish anxiety
- Create a bond

This, in sales, is the essence of what building **rapport** is all about. **The bonus is that rapport leads to trust.** Yes, we trust people with whom we have something in common.

Though building rapport is easier with people whom you naturally and obviously *have* something in common with, the real skill comes into play when you are able to build rapport with everyone. So in sales today you must be able to *find* the commonality or, if one does not exist, you must be able to *create* the commonality.

Finding the Commonality

Fortunately, women naturally tend to communicate with others by way of seeking out rapport connections, as Deborah

Tannen notes in her best-seller on male/female communication, *You Just Don't Understand*. Women place emphasis on similar experiences, and relate to others through commonalities. In other words, they instinctively understand the means to quickly establish rapport and are very comfortable engaging in that process. It is part of their communication style.

One just has to listen to women in conversation to become aware of their rapport-building skills. It won't take long before you hear the references to shared experiences and attempts to relate. "I know what you mean," "I have that very problem," "Me too," "Same here," and "I went through the identical thing" are commonly heard phrases that emphasize a woman's desire to bond with others through like experiences.

So now you know that women are interested in commonalities and are quick to bring them to light in conversation. But how do you use this gift in sales? Quite simply, use your natural curiosity to find out what you have in common with your prospect. Find it as quickly as you can. Realize it can be anything. It can be something as simple as the fact that you were both born in July, that you both have two children, that you both have relatives from Poughkeepsie, that you both love anchovies, or that you both have trouble driving a stick shift car.

If this does not come about naturally, be smart and introduce subjects into the conversation that have the potential for surfacing the common experience. Topics such as:

- Hobbies
- Travel experiences
- Aspirations
- Children
- Social interests
- Educational values
- Sports
- Mutual acquaintances

- Professional associations
- Recreational activities

are good ones to launch you on surfacing the commonalities that will provide that rapport-building opportunity.

Once you have uncovered the similarity, find ways to allude to it during the course of your presentation. It just has to surface once or twice during your time together for that unconscious affinity and subconscious loyalty to take hold. Rapport is created and as a result, that prospect will most likely prefer to deal with you instead of someone else. This is the groundwork, the foundation, the essence for building trust. Remember: **Rapport leads to trust,** an essential in today's business world.

Creating the Similarities

Uncovering commonalities creates a feeling of similarity (she is just like me), but there are other verbal and even physical ways to create a feeling of similarity that also enhance a feeling of rapport.

Verbal Techniques

You now understand that we feel more comfortable with people who can relate to our experiences. But did you know that we also feel more comfortable with people who actually *talk the way we talk,* as well as with people who appear to *think the way we think?* Let's look into how we can expand our rapport, building skills by verbally paralleling our customers in terms of *talking patterns* and/or *thinking patterns.*

TALKING PATTERNS

When I deplane in Biloxi, Mississippi, an amazing thing happens ... I develop a southern accent. I use the term "y'all" as if it were second nature. It doesn't stop here. Entering a taxi at Heathrow en route to my hotel in London, I quite comfortably greet the driver with "cheerio" and use the phrase "jolly well" at least three times in conversation. I don't think that I am the only one who falls into this language patterning. But I do know why it happens.

Certainly it is not that I think that my southern or British accent is authentic enough to fool anyone. My purpose is not to pull the wool over someone's eyes. My purpose is to fit in. Not only do I want to feel more comfortable, I want the person I am speaking with to more readily accept me. This clearly demonstrates an important point. We unconsciously know that people are more comfortable being around people who talk like them.

I am not advising that you master a Brooklyn accent when you are selling in Manhattan or a Cajun twang when selling to Pierre LaFonte from New Orleans. But I am strongly suggesting that you understand the benefits of matching the way you speak in some way with your customer's style as it creates a similarity that will lead to an enhanced feeling of rapport.

Women can do this quite easily. First of all, we as a gender are able to handle verbal material better than men. Women are known to have keener language skills than men and quite simply are more tuned in to verbal communication. Women are more interested in language than men. This is substantiated by the fact that the number of advanced degrees given out to women in the field of language is almost double those given out to men.

As such, your ability as a woman to excel at verbal tasks will make you better able to understand verbal paralleling, and it will make it easier for you to incorporate those skills into your sales repertoire.

In a sales situation it is critical to listen to the specific words your prospect uses. All people have favorite words—words that for them have special meaning. The key here is to pick up on these words and incorporate them in your sales presentation. Sometimes this involves dropping a similar word that may be your favorite, and inserting your customer's word instead. Consider this scenario:

CUSTOMER: "I want a machine that is dependable."
SALESPERSON: "This machine is very reliable."

This salesperson is not speaking to his customer. Although the concept discussed is the same, and although you perhaps interpret the word "reliable" as meaning the same thing as "dependable," the prospect may not. The prospect obviously relates to the word "dependable," and that is the key. A smart salesperson would pick up on this and parallel the customer's choice of wording by using her word—the word "dependable." Consider this scenario:

CUSTOMER: "I want to move into a home that is spacious and open."

SALESPERSON: "Then you'll love this home. It's nice and roomy and very large."

Here again, the salesperson is not speaking the customer's language. Although the words "roomy" and "large" may mean open and spacious to the salesperson, and may even be thought of by the customer as synonyms, why not hedge your bets? You will definitely be right on the mark, know you are talking her language, increase the impact of your message, and demonstrate a commonality with your client if you use his words.

Like anything else, you must use common sense in executing this technique for creating the commonality that can lead to rapport. You don't want this to come off as "parroting" or mimicking, as that will work to your disadvantage and could actually kill rapport.

Armed with this little bit of knowledge and with some thinking and practice, you will soon be able to make this sound quite natural by skipping a few beats in the conversation and inserting the right word (your customer's word) a few minutes later in the presentation.

A word of caution, however. Since we are aiming for rapport as an outgrowth of this technique, and since rapport in this case must be positive, we should use paralleling only in a positive way. Therefore, those words or phrases of the customer's you choose to parallel or duplicate should be positive, upbeat, and favorable. You should avoid using this technique to duplicate anything that can be construed as, or reinforce, a negative. For example:

CUSTOMER: "We are not interested in buying a television that is too expensive."

SALESPERSON: "Well, here's a TV that is not too expensive."

Using the consumer's words in this case can intimate that the product you are now showing her is cheap. Instead it would be wise to rephrase the consumer's words to:

SALESPERSON: "Well, here's a TV with an outstanding sales price."

Another thought with regard to paralleling: It does not have to occur only when talking about the product. It is a technique that can be incorporated all throughout the conversation track. In fact, since rapport is one of the first goals in a sales encounter, most likely your initial opportunity to employ paralleling will occur while engaging in causal nonproduct-oriented conversation.

THINKING PATTERNS

Everyone does not perceive or think things through in the same manner. People do not all understand, absorb, relate, or react to words, phrases, or concepts in the same way. It has been proven that rapport with any prospect can be magnified significantly if you, as a salesperson, are able to talk in the same perceptual language as your prospect thinks.

How do you know how she thinks? Neurolingustic programming (NLP) is a relatively new science that studies how we can use language to program or condition our own brains as well as the brains of others to better relate, influence, and get what we want.

According to the theory of NLP, there are three primary ways that individuals perceive the world:

- Visually
- Auditorily
- Kinesthetically

Most people you encounter will reveal the thinking category that they personally fall into through the words that they speak and the eye movements that they favor.

The Visual Person

Visually oriented people think in terms of pictures. They are more sensitive to, and relate better to, the visual environment than to sounds and feelings.

Speaking patterns:

They use words like: see, picture, look, watch, focus, imagine, envision, reflect, scan, and glance.

They use phrases like: in view of, it appears to me, I can plainly see, it looks like, in light of, scope it out, eye to eye, etc.

Eye movement patterns:

The visualizer's tendency is to look upward when thinking about, digesting, or relating to information. Most people will look up naturally if asked to picture something. It is just that visualizers favor this form of thinking, and you can see it in their eyes.

The Auditory Person

Auditorily oriented people are more sound-oriented. They relate well to, and tend to focus in on, sounds, words, voices that surround them. Pictures and feelings are less appealing for them to relate to.

Speaking patterns:

They use words like: hear, listen, attune, sounds, harmonize, silence, rings, and utterly.

They use phrases like: clear as a bell, express yourself, tell me, sounds good to me, I hear you loud and clear, voice an opinion, what an earful, state your purpose, etc.

Eye movement patterns:

The auditory person's tendency is to look to the side when thinking about, digesting, or relating to information. Most people will look laterally naturally when asked to recall or construct a sound. It is just that auditorily oriented people favor this form of thinking, and you can see it in their eyes.

The Kinesthetic Person

Kinesthetically oriented people think in terms of feelings. These feelings can be either emotional or tactile, or both. These are the type of people who buy something because it feels right, like someone because there are good vibes, and tend to follow their "gut" instincts.

Speaking patterns:

They use words like: feel, touch, grasp, concrete, hard, solid, hold, and guts.

They use phrases like: make contact, get a handle on, get in touch with, hang in there, hand in hand, pain in the neck, pull some strings, sharp as a tack, come to grips with, etc.

Eye movement patterns:

Kinesthetic people have a tendency to look downward and to their right when thinking about, digesting, or relating to information. Most people will look down and to their right naturally when asked to recall or construct a feeling. It is just that the kinesthetic person favors this form of thinking, and you can see it in their eyes.

Effective use of NLP requires astute listening skills and finely tuned observation skills, along with a genuine interest in relating to others and in being understood. Women, as detailed later on in this book, possess superior listening and observation skills. Additionally, women have proven to have more of an interest in creating harmony. You can easily see why women, with an understanding of the concepts behind NLP, can smoothly implement the preceding techniques to advantage in the selling arena.

The key is to listen and watch for the clues that will allow you to make an assessment of which way of thinking your prospect favors. Though some people may be more difficult to peg in this manner than others, and though some may seem to use a combination of styles, in 90 percent of your client contact, using NLP techniques will really help you to establish rapport. Through listening and watching, you will be able to determine the way your clients think and adjust your verbal presentation style to match their way of thinking and better relate to them. For example:

- **Visual Sales Talk**—"Can't you just picture," "Can't you just imagine," "Can't you see," "Just envision how this phone system can make your life easier." "Take a look at this brochure," "See these testimonial letters." "Imagine how much better your reports will look."

- **Auditory Sales Talk**—"Let me tell you all about it," "Talk to me about your needs." "This product speaks for itself," "Is this in tune with what you are thinking?" "Let me hear your concerns." "Doesn't it sound like your company could really benefit from this?"

- **Kinesthetic Sales Talk**—"It has to feel right, doesn't it?" "It's important to grasp the concept," "Hold on to that thought," "I want to stay in touch with you," "I know you don't want to fumble around with this decision," "You seem able to grasp that quite easily." "You have a gut sense that this is the way to go, don't you?"

Remember our aim here is to create a common feeling, an essence of comfort, and an environment that will bring about a feeling of rapport.

Physical Techniques

Getting in step with people physically is one of the most overlooked, yet most powerful, ways to create an air of commonality and a feeling of similarity. There are two subtle yet effective means to get your prospect aligned with you: *physical pacing* and *mirroring/matching*.

PHYSICAL PACING

Think about shopping with a girlfriend. Covering ground in a shopping mall is the primary way I get my exercise. We talk, we chat, we snack, we spend, and we walk. Boy, do we walk! Have you ever noticed, however, that sometimes when you are walking and talking, the conversation just flows? Words come easily. Thoughts spill out and there seems to be no end to the banter. Next time your "walkin' and talkin'" feels this good . . . look down. I bet that you and your friend are in step; in other words, when you're on your right foot, she's on her right foot, when you're on your left, she's on her left. You're walking in beat. Funny how that affects the conversation flow.

Being in physical step with each other actually promotes easier conversation. I think we women know this instinctively. Because on those rare occasions when we get out of step, we quickly, upon realizing it, do that little "catch-up move." You know that little step, a shuffle-skip combo that gets you back on the correct foot, so you can walk in beat with your friend.

Now, just because I am talking about two women here doesn't mean that you can't use this walking-in-step pattern to enhance your conversation with a man. It works just as well. However, if your conversation with him gets out of sync, and you look down and notice that you are out of step, don't ever count on the man to do that little "catch-up thing," that shuffle-skip combo move to get you back in harmony. Nope, men don't do this. I don't think they even know about it. But women do it for a reason, and that reason is sound. Women are very attuned to physical pacing and even sometimes on an unconscious level search for ways to create a physical harmony with the person with whom they are trying to communicate.

In sales, getting physically in sync with your prospect can be accomplished quite easily. It can be a big factor in communicating your interest in building rapport. It unconsciously sends a powerful affirmation to your prospects that you are in beat with them, concerned about them, tuned in to them, and seek a harmonious relationship.

Physical pacing has to do with matching to your prospect's pace the way you move when gesturing, walking, or changing positions. Naturally, we must use our observation skills to pick up the prospect's pace to begin with, but once that is done, all we have to do is make a conscious effort to slow down or speed up accordingly. For example: If you are taking a prospect on a tour of the plant, stay in step. Resist the urge to lead the way by being ten paces ahead or to lag behind to give him space. Keep a comfortable distance, don't crowd, but align yourself and stay in pace.

Even when gesticulating, physical pacing comes into play. Don't flag your arms emphatically if that is not your prospect's style. Doing so can create an almost threatening environment for some people. I recall seeing a very unanimated customer duck several times during a presentation with a very dramatic salesperson.

Some of the most persuasive people in the world today (negotiators, politicians, attorneys) study the benefits of the pacing technique and sometimes carry it to the limit. I've seen some of the best of the best actually match their breathing patterns to those of the people they are trying to persuade, motivate, win over, or sway.

Although I wouldn't advocate carrying breath matching to a great extreme, I have seen it used effectively during the pauses in a sales presentation. While silently waiting for a customer's answer or reaction, you can duplicate her breathing pattern, and still be selling by creating an atmosphere conducive to rapport.

Before moving on, it must be recognized that keeping in pace with your prospect can also be applied to the verbal portion of your presentation. The tendency in sales, when one gets to know the product very well, is to speak quite rapidly, as that seems to imply confidence. The key, however, is to again register the speed of speech your client uses and match this the best you can. This simple adjustment will give your customer the impression that you are similar. That similarity creates an ease. As a rule of thumb I advocate a snappy moderate pace most of the time, but remember to speed up or slow down according to your prospect's conversational speaking style.

MIRRORING AND MATCHING

Mirroring and matching are techniques that again require astute observation skills. They involve watching the bits of body language your prospect uses and then either mirror-imaging or matching the gestures discreetly. These simple techniques, when used with finesse, have been widely accepted as a means to create that feeling of similarity and deepen rapport in an unobtrusive and natural manner.

For example, you are sitting face-to-face with your prospect and she crosses her left ankle over her right. You are matching your customer if you make the identical movement. But you are mirroring her if you cross your right ankle over your left (i.e., creating the mirror image). Again, using simple techniques like this in the sales arena creates and fosters that comfort zone, that feeling of likeness that is the prerequisite for rapport and the foundation of trust.

As you can see, there are many ways to capitalize on this first rule of trust and to use this in the selling arena to start your association with each and every prospect off on the right foot. Now let's move on to the second rule of trust.

WE TEND TO TRUST PEOPLE WITH WHOM WE CAN AGREE

Creating a basis for agreement:

SOLIDIFIES CREDIBILITY
ENHANCES CONVERSATIONAL FLOW
INSTILLS CONFIDENCE
INCREASES THE LEVEL OF TRUST

The technique of creating agreement is also used deliberately by astute negotiators worldwide. Actually, persuasive people in general seem to employ this technique quite naturally in dealing with others. Think about politicians, advertising copywriters—even comedians. No matter what the source, the results are powerful.

The hypnotist is a perfect example of someone who relies on the creation of an agreement base to treat clients. The hypnotist uses agreement to place clients in a receptive frame of mind, to establish trust, and eventually to gain control. Let's examine the method the hypnotist uses, so we can discover how a sense of agreement and trust is created as quickly as possible.

Several years ago I was smoking about three packs of cigarettes a day. I really loved to smoke, but everyone around me was driving me nuts. My family criticized me with every puff. Eventually I started to smoke cigarettes on the sneak—in the garage, in the bathroom—just as I had done when I was teenager. Intellectually, I knew I should stop, but I couldn't seem to kick the habit. I tried nicotine gum, Smokenders, Life-Savers, cigarette holders, sitting on my hands—but nothing worked.

An ex-smoker friend of mine convinced me that hypnosis had worked for her. In desperation, I decided to try it. I phoned the recommended hypnotist's office on a Tuesday and spoke with his receptionist. We made an appointment for Friday morning at ten-thirty.

I arrived at the appointed time and took a seat in the waiting room. I was called in by the hypnotist himself, who greeted me with a warm smile. Realizing—now—that we tend to trust people we can agree with, I understand why the initial conversation went something like this:

HYPNOTIST: "Your name is Nicki Joy?"

ME: "Yes."

HYPNOTIST: "I see that you called my office Tuesday and spoke with my receptionist, is that right?"

ME: "That's right."

HYPNOTIST: "And you made an appointment for today, Friday, at ten-thirty, correct?"

ME: "Correct."

HYPNOTIST: "And here you are?"

ME: "Yes, here I am."

HYPNOTIST: "Would you like to come in and take a seat?"

ME: "Sure."

HYPNOTIST: "Nicki, I see you have a little problem."

ME: "Yes, I do."

HYPNOTIST: "And I see that problem is smoking, am I right?"

ME: "You're right."

HYPNOTIST: "And you're hoping that perhaps hypnosis can help you?"

ME: "That's right."

HYPNOTIST: "Now, I see you were recommended by your friend Rhonda VanCleff?"

ME: "Yes."

HYPNOTIST: "Nicki?"

ME: "Yes."

HYPNOTIST: "Are you ready?"

    ME: "Yes, I'm ready."

HYPNOTIST: "Nicki?"

    ME: "Uh-huh?"

HYPNOTIST: "You are listening to the sound of my voice."

    ME: "Uh-huh."

HYPNOTIST: "And your eyelids are getting heavy."

    ME: *Snoring sound* . . . (not only were my eyelids getting heavy . . . but in two minutes I was snoring and drooling)

I don't know if you've been counting, but so far I have said "yes" to this man, in one form or another, thirteen times. Now, my subconscious mind grabbed on to that fact before my conscious mind did. So when he spoke his last sentence, "You are listening to the sound of my voice and your eyelids are getting heavy," I subconsciously thought, "This guy has been right thirteen times so far, he must be right now."

Very simply, the hypnotist established a reputation for speaking the truth. From the start he asked me questions that had only one answer—"Yes." Once he had gained my conscious acceptance of him as a truth teller, he capitalized on that credibility to plant a suggestion that I would accept as fact. When he told me that my eyelids were getting heavy, I believed him. My unconscious took over and my eyelids even *felt* heavy.

This technique demonstrates a savvy use of truth statements. Truth statements are little questions specifically geared to get a "yes" response. They were used by my hypnotist to establish his credibility, instill a sense of trust, and place him in a position of control. Good salespeople use this same technique.

Women seek agreement naturally. This may be because women, more so than men, generally make a greater effort to avoid conflict. Men are not as intent on agreeing and value their independence and differences more. Women, however, are skilled at phrasing questions to achieve agreement. Before moving to a new point or topic, women have a tendency to seek agreement with their listeners. "Don't you think so?" "Right?" "You know?" Women work hard to create connections, find similarities, and seek agreement as a means of creating rapport.

Moving this propensity into the sales arena, you can begin to create a yes momentum by asking questions . . . loaded questions . . . certain to elicit a "yes" response. Though this needs to be planned, it works like a charm.

Simple truth statements should be used up front in your presentation to begin creating an agreement base. For example, "I see you received the brochure I sent you last week," or "I imagine you want all the information as quickly as possible," or "I know up to this point you have used another service," or "It looks like the rain finally stopped, right?"

Though you must use this technique subtly, the more "yeses" you manage to elicit, the more solid your agreement base. You are establishing a reputation for speaking the truth, and soon the listener will have a tendency to accept even your *suggestion* as the truth. Talk about trust. Talk about control.

"Your contract with XYZ Company ends in October; you should sign up with us now." This sentence is structured the same as "You're listening to the sound of my voice and your eyelids are getting heavy." The first part of the sentence is an indisputable truth, the second part is a suggestion. But remember, by establishing enough truths up front, the suggestion you launch into can become fact.

(It should be noted that a "no" response that is shared with a customer may on the surface seem to provide the same feeling of agreement—but it does not. For example: "You don't want to buy a dishwasher that will break in a year, do you?" In actuality this approach can come off as demeaning to the customer; it fails to use the power of the "yes" momentum and is just not as effective.)

In sales, establishing a level of trust places you in a position to direct the course of the presentation. The client who trusts you will listen more carefully to your words, allow you the time to present your product, and will be less likely to disagree with your message. And the bond you create with your client will dramatically increase your chances to make the sale.

In sales, trust is something that is earned. However, a feeling of trust can be cultivated by your efforts in establishing agreement and in developing a sense of rapport with your customer. Women seek agreement naturally and try hard to find rapport connections with others. This is the glue that creates strong bonds.

3

LITTLE THINGS MEAN A LOT

□ □ □

REASON #3
Women Get the Details Down

In sales, it's the little things that are often over-looked that count. Women are prone to take the little things into account—and naturally excel at many of the details that have proven to be essential to good selling.

I n sales, when there is time, the salesperson should "woo" the prospect; when time is limited, the salesperson must "wow" the prospect. Both involve doing the little things. As in love, where "wooing and wowing" is the name of the game, **in sales it's the little things that count.**

It is the little things that can make the difference between a memorable experience and a fleeting encounter. It's the little things, such as acknowledging special occasions, returning phone calls on time, remembering people's names, etc., that demonstrate interest and effort, and encourage the consumer to want to deal with you and only you. And it's often the little things that are neglected and overlooked by busy salespeople who are so focused on winning that they forget how to play the game.

In sales it has been proven that **to get big, you must think small.** You see, selling is a process. And getting your customer to buy what you are selling is not something that happens at a specific moment or point in time, it is instead a result of the cumulative effort of all the little things you do well during the course of the sale. The key, therefore, is to first recognize the importance of these little things, make certain they are a part of each and every sales encounter, and then perfect them so that they indeed have the impact that they should.

Salespeople are always being reminded by sales trainers to "go back to the basics." It is important that we understand that the little things *are* the basics. Unfortunately, many "seasoned" salespeople lose touch because they skip steps, take shortcuts, and underestimate or ignore the importance of the little things. There is a tendency when sales are booming to think the little things *don't* matter, and there is a tendency when sales are faltering to think the little things *won't* matter. This thinking is wrong!

We must remember, as the saying goes, that we don't stumble over the mountains; it is the pebbles that trip us up in life. In sales, too, it is the pebbles, i.e., the details of selling, that we have to watch out for. And details—who is better at looking after the details than women?

- Have you ever noticed that if a man suggests to a woman that they go camping for the weekend, it is the woman who thinks about putting the dog in the kennel, packing warm clothes just in case, canceling the newspaper, unplugging the coffeepot, and taking along the insect repellant? Men concentrate on the big picture; women take care of the details.

- Have you ever noticed that a man may suggest a Fourth of July barbecue for all the friends? He may even get the coals working, cook the burgers, and buy the beer. But it is the woman who thinks of sending the invitations, buying the napkins, cups, and forks, deciding on a menu, coming up with a rain date, and borrowing the industrial-size coffeepot from the neighbor. Men concentrate on the big picture; women take care of the details.

- Have you ever noticed that a man can easily make a big-picture decision to move his father to Florida? But it is the woman who scouts out possible condos, makes sure the furniture will fit, checks out the closet space, arranges for the phone hookup and utility installations, and gets the change-of-address cards printed. Men concentrate on the big picture; women take care of the details.

I guarantee the position of a secretary was conceived of by a businessman to handle his details. And ever since women infiltrated the workplace after WWII, you'll note he rarely hired a man for the job. It is a fact that the original role of a wife involved taking care of the small occurrences of everyday life. And I am certain, though I have no historical proof to support this, that when Adam and Eve finished that apple, it was Eve who figured out what to do with the core and the pits.

Though details might seem minor, their importance is major, in life and in sales. In fact, the ability to handle the details is very desirable. In a business scenario it often makes the detail handler indispensable. In a personal relationship, this ability creates reliance as well and a sense of worth. And in sales, this ability establishes an image of sensitivity, awareness, professionalism, attentiveness, common sense, refinement, and value.

One of the attributes of consistently top-notch salespeople is their determination to belabor the obvious and their dedication to paying special attention to little activities and details, that keep customers happy and provide them with the kind of service, attention, and reassurance they need. One can easily see why women would be great at work details such as tracking inventory on a routine basis and checking the stock of supplies and printed literature needed to sell (no different really from making sure that there is enough toothpaste in the tube and milk in the fridge), keeping precise notations as to what transpired during the last contact with the client (no different really from keeping that teenage diary), maintaining accurate and neat sales records (no different really from maintaining the family's dental and health records), collecting (on an ongoing basis) testimonial and reference letters from happy clients (no different really from collecting good report cards, sports awards, and A+ papers), etc. Get the picture?

Yes, although details may seem inconsequential, in actuality they make a major difference in the way you are perceived and received by the customer as well as by your company. In sales it is the little things that make the big things happen.

Now, by highlighting the importance of details in sales, I am not suggesting that you forget the big picture, your objective and your goal. **It is just that to get more income from sales, you have to be less obsessed about the outcome and more focused on the ingredients that help to make it all happen.** It helps that women don't get "mired by minutiae" and actually have the ability to look at the big picture as well as the small one.

So let's take a look at a few other little details of selling, the nuances and subtleties that comprise some of the very basics of the business and help propel you on a path of success.

THE SMILE

Anyone in sales—except perhaps those in the funeral business—realizes the importance of smiling. In fact, nothing says "acceptance" like a smile. It also says "success." That's right, a smile is an outward manifestation of inward cheerfulness, and cheerfulness is associated with success. If a salesperson smiles, one thinks, "Boy, business must be great." If he or she is sullen or dour, one thinks, "Boy, business must be lousy." Since most people feel more confident buying from someone who is already successful, the smile is the first essential in the business of selling.

You should also know that, besides making people appear to be successful, a smile makes people appear more attractive. Furthermore, people who smile are perceived by others to be more credible than those with more constrained facial expressions.

Smiling is an obvious detail. However, it is often ignored by those with a great deal of experience, who forget the importance of this little effort, disregard the small steps that lead to big results, and underestimate the impact a smile has on others.

As cited by Jane Barr Stump, Ph.D., in her book, *What's the Difference? How Men and Women Compare,* women are attributed with smiling more than men. Additionally, research has suggested that female infants smile reflexively as a result of their heightened sensitivity to external stimuli such as light, sound, and touch. Though a reflexive smile is different from the more social smile that develops later, many agree that the reflexive smile actually prepares the path to the social smile.

EYE CONTACT

"Look at me when I'm talking to you" is a reprimand most of us have heard from early childhood. Why is looking at someone, giving someone eye contact, so important when he or she is talking? It indicates interest and receptivity. It indicates that the message is getting across.

Though intellectually most of us are aware that eye contact does not necessarily indicate involvement, it still serves to create the impression of listening, understanding, and caring. Good eye contact is such a convincing body language signal that it can even be used to fake interest. I mastered this in college during my earth science classes.

Since sales involves getting your message across as well as demonstrating receptivity and interest, look at someone when she is talking. In sales, listening, understanding and caring **must occur on a genuine level;** however, a quick route to convey that message is through the use of good eye contact.

Now, by eye contact, I am not referring to staring down the individual. In fact, when carried to an extreme, eye contact can intimate aggression and actually dehumanize the encounter. But when used sensibly, eye contact will not only convey a positive impression of you, but will encourage your customer to be as focused on you as you are on her. Simply put, if you are comfortable providing eye contact, chances are the person you are talking to will be more comfortable returning it.

Guess what. "Females are superior at making and maintaining eye contact, beginning in the cradle,'' according to *Newsweek* magazine. Communication patterns are formed at an early age, when boys spend more time talking to boys, and girls spend more time talking to girls.

In fact, as Deborah Tannen's research reveals in *You Just Don't Understand,* the posturing of men when engaged in conversation with other men makes eye contact more difficult for them to achieve. Females tend to position themselves in a way that allows them to look at other females comfortably and directly. Males, on the other hand, sit at angles to one another and avoid each other's eyes. Furthermore, females fix their eyes on one another during conversation and look around only once in a while. Males, however, tend to operate in just the reverse manner, by fixing their eyes on inanimate objects in the room and shifting eye contact and attention back to the other person once in a while. However, from observing scenarios between female salespeople and male customers for twenty years, I've noticed that men are more likely to adjust their eye contact to the female pattern rather than the reverse.

Eye contact is clearly another small detail that really counts in sales—another small detail that women not only can master but in which they already have the edge.

USING A CLIENT'S NAME

Another obvious basic that falls through the cracks involves using the client's name during the course of your sales encounter. It doesn't take a rocket scientist to know that people like to hear their own name. They feel flattered if you remember it and respected when you use it.

So why is it that salespeople who know this fact intellectually often let this little nuance drift out of their repertoire? Probably because they feel they have more important issues to concentrate on. *You don't.* Using someone's name helps create a ''comfort level,'' a necessary prelude to the sale.

The airlines know this. Whenever I take off from Washington National Airport, as we are pulling away from the gate, the message from the flight attendant over the PA system sounds something like this: "Ladies and gentlemen, thank you for flying Delta Airlines. In one hour and thirty-eight minutes we will be landing at Atlanta's Hartsfield International Airport. And flying this Boeing 727 today is Captain Pete McDonald."

Now, why do they tell me that? I don't turn to the person seated next to me and comment, "Oh, he's good." When I deplane I don't say, "Thanks, Pete. Great flight!" I don't write to Delta to report Pete's excellent landing. Why do they introduce him? Because they know that this simple act of identifying the captain by name creates credibility, trust, a feeling of personalized service, and a comfort level.

Surprisingly, it also benefits Pete and Delta, too. You see, when Pete, in the flight deck, hears his own name, he pays attention and feels a heightened sense of accountability. Bottom line, this simple little introduction makes Pete perform better.

Again, it is important to engage in this "name calling" with discretion. Using a prospect's name too much during the course of the presentation comes off as a manipulative technique, exercised for the sole purpose of proving that you remembered the name. It comes off as phony—slick and insincere.

I have found that **top sales professionals have a tendency to use the customer's name three to four times during the course of an hour to an hour-and-fifteen-minute presentation.** Top sales professionals also recognize the importance of learning and using the name of any support staff personnel they come in contact with, whether by phone or in person. Not only will those people, who often feel a sense of anonymity, remember you, but they will make more of an effort to help you at every turn.

Remembering someone's name is an essential in business, but calling a person by the wrong name can kill your credibility—in a flash. Therefore, if you have the gift for name remembering, be thankful, and if you don't, you'd better develop it. Before I learned how to remember names, I used to try to avoid embarrassing situations, by quipping, "I'm so sorry, I just forgot your first—and last name."

Mnemonics is a system used to improve memory or recall through an association technique, and it has helped me immeasurably. Any book on improving memory talks about mnemonics and can easily teach you the art of visual association that works especially well when trying to remember names.

Basically, you formulate picture associations. If you meet someone named Harry Snow, you immediately repeat the name verbally, then mentally, following up by creatively conjuring up an association picture. The most bizarre pictures work the best to trigger recall, e.g., a hairy snowman. Say you are introduced to Roberta Stockman. Your picture might be a female robber with a stocking over her head, which makes her look like a man.

Mnemonics is a topic unto itself, but a system that can be quickly mastered and one that will give you immediate results. In fact, after a while it can actually become second nature to you.

THE HUMAN TOUCH

The "human touch" is a difficult thing to define as it relates to the sales encounter. But it is a part of the selling process that is essential. It diffuses the negative stereotype of selling as being coercive, manipulative, detached, impersonal, and self-serving. The "human touch" as it relates to sales consists of increasing your awareness and acknowledging the more personal side of your client's life, while helping her to buy what you are selling.

Selling today is more than strictly business. Our business and personal lives are quite complex and tend to mesh together, even for those with a great ability to separate. Being sensitive to your clients as total human beings does not mean that you have to get personal with them. What it does mean, however, is that you are sensitive, alert, and caring about the personal issues that impact and influence your customers' lives.

Incorporating the "human touch" has to do with demonstrating your interest and awareness in those aspects of your client's life that lie outside the business world but that are obviously important to her. Your interest will result in a stronger client/salesperson bond; it will ingratiate you to your client and set you apart as unique. It requires astute listening and observation skills and then the ability to incorporate what you learn casually but with interest into your interaction with the client.

Women have a natural sensitivity to, and an understanding of, the fact that there is life *outside* the business arena that affects what happens *in* the business arena.

This feminine awareness may be due to women's own multiple roles as businesspeople, wives, and mothers. Women's ability to then capitalize on this sensitivity may also be an aspect of their nurturing instinct, which involves creating a comfort level for people with whom they interact.

If, in the past, women have been criticized for bringing the personal world into the business world, it is not the case anymore. The fact is that the high-tech world we live in has created a need for "high touch." John Nesbitt, author of *Megatrends,* as well as other modern business gurus, saw this coming. They warned us all that high technology would do more to isolate the individual physically from his or her fellow man than to bring them together (working, banking, and shopping at home via computers and modems, advanced telecommunication systems replacing the need for in-person meetings, etc.). They were right, and the backlash in business has already begun with an emphasis on a more personal approach—an approach that is right up a woman's alley.

Though selling with a human touch must be done with a high degree of common sense, tact, and discretion, it can serve to provide important insight into the buyer, foster a personal bond, and generate good feelings that compensate both parties in some way for the lack of human contact brought about by our high-tech world. Most companies are getting on the bandwagon and believe that their longevity and competitive edge will come from their ability to incorporate that human touch in the workplace. An account executive for one of the top corporations in America today,

Marriott, told me confidentially that the push is on from the top, and the message is loud and clear, to get out there and relate to clients on a more personal level. Mixing business with pleasure is no longer only relegated to a shared interest in golf.

You can gain a great deal of insight into the client's interests and "outside" life by noticing:

- Photos on the desk
- Diplomas on the wall
- Trophies on the shelves
- Types of plants on the window ledge

You can position yourself for more "human touch" conversation with your client by registering:

- Birthdays
- Sports interests of their children
- Hobbies
- Family member names

Questions like "How did your son's soccer game go?" "How was your daughter, Nancy, in the play?" "Is your mother feeling better?" "Are you settled in your new home yet?" "Did you firm up the dates for your vacation in Maine?" and "How's the new car running?" show your interest, caring, and understanding that we do not live in a business-isolated world. This "human touch" effort by you will be appreciated by both men and women and can differentiate you from other salespeople.

Doing this might sound easy, especially for a woman since, as convention has it, we seem to have a natural affinity to be more interested in the personal details of people's lives than men. However, when you are dealing with many customers at once, it may be difficult to keep all the details and information straight.

Most successful salespeople, therefore, keep a three-by-five card catalog just for this purpose. Each client is indexed on a card, where you record the personal information you've learned. Before each visit, review the card, update it after the visit, and use the information to further solidify the salesperson/customer bond.

If you are fortunate enough to work for a company that provides you with a computer, there are many software programs to help you keep tabs on your customers easily.

Yes, it is the details. Yes, it is the little things that mean a lot. All these little things together have great impact.

Behavioral scientists have guesstimated that we spend seven years of our lives in the bathroom (some of us spend longer), six years eating (some of us spend longer), five years waiting in line, four years cleaning our homes (some of us spend shorter—they didn't poll me when they came up with that one), three years attending unnecessary meetings, two years looking for things that we lost, one year on hold, eight months sitting at red lights, six months opening and throwing away junk mail . . . and the list goes on.

Now, even if those figures don't accurately represent your particular lifestyle, there is a message here. Life is cumulative and we do indeed measure out our lives in teaspoons of small actions and activities.

The business of sales is cumulative, too, and you will, in fact, measure out your success based on how you perfect the small actions and activities involved in the process.

– 4 –
IT'S ALARMING HOW CHARMING I FEEL (OR THE HITCHHIKER'S DRESS CODE)

❑ ❑ ❑

REASON #4
Women Are Good at Looking Good

Looking good is the first step in creating the impression of being good. Women have been working on looking good forever. Looking good in the sales arena establishes the face validity needed to start the sale off right.

I've always wondered why it is that hitchhikers don't dress better. Don't they know, when they get up in the morning, that they don't have a car? Don't they understand that they're going to need a ride? Don't they realize, as they are dressing, that to get to where they want to go, they are going to have to look good enough to get someone's positive attention and win over someone's confidence? Why don't they make some effort to cover the tattoo that reads "Born to Kill" and to wear the "Charles Manson fan club T-shirt" *under,* let's say, an oxford button-down? It's obvious that hitchhikers don't have the first clue about the concept of *Face Validity.*

Face Validity refers to the fact that in our society we have come to believe that if it looks good . . . it is good. Yes, America has come to believe that if it dazzles, it must be diamonds; if it glitters, it must be gold.

Now, I doubt that many hitchhikers will pick up this book

and get this message. But isn't it a shame that they are unaware of the concept of creating face validity, the benefit of personal packaging to:

- Predispose a positive impression
- Gain favorable attention
- Win over someone's initial confidence

If hitchhikers understood that, I *know* they'd get to where they want to go quicker. The same is true in sales! If you understand the importance of *packaging yourself* for positive predisposition and favorable attention . . . you, too, can get to where you want to go quicker.

Yes, creating a positive first impression, via packaging, works for both products and people. If you want someone to stop, take notice, and make a positive first assessment of you, you better come off as looking good, because *looking good is the first step in creating the image of being good.* It is the first step in creating a quick *image of worth.*

Think about the candy sold at the movies. They charge three dollars for a fifty cent box of candy. What, are they crazy? Who would pay that outrageous price? True, they have a captive audience, and true, just purchasing a ticket often triggers your sweet tooth, but have you also noticed that the candy selection is lined up in a glass jewelry display case? The movie people help the candy-purchase process along through *packaging.* The Raisinets are propped up on black velvet. It makes me feel that I should approach the counter and say, "I'd like to see something in a Milk Dud, please." In their own way, through product presentation and packaging, sellers of overpriced candy at movie counters are portraying an image of worth.

Marketing specialists all over the world know the value of packaging. In fact, market research proves over and over that the majority of people cannot distinguish between Pepsi and Coke, Folgers and Maxwell House, or Minute Maid and Donald Duck orange juice when the label is covered. Research has even shown that orange juice seems to taste better to most people when it is served from cartons with a brighter orange color, and eggs are likely to taste better from a carton labeled "farm fresh" rather than from cartons just labeled "grade A." Yes, exterior packaging, establishing face validity, is the first step in winning 'em over. As Carolyn Corbin reinforces in *Strategies 2000,* in the final analysis, the most appealing package will not compensate for a bad-quality product, but it does have a great impact on initial preference and selection.

In an era when products and people have a shorter shelf life than ever before, drawing positive attention to yourself quickly constitutes a very important competitive edge. Those who have the ability to package themselves well will get immediate attention, the first shot, and most importantly, establish an *up-front image of credibility and worth.*

Understanding this is critical. If your customers are not attracted to you very quickly, your chances of capturing their interest are nearly nil. There is no doubt that during the first two to four minutes of contact:

- The customer forms opinions that will be difficult to dispel
- The customer's attention span is the most intense
- The customer's ability to retain information is at its peak

People concentrate first on what they can *see.* So before you even open your mouth to speak, half of your total message is already conveyed. Understanding this concept in the selling arena enables you to see why physical packaging and image projection must be orchestrated to create appeal, encourage initial attention, and generate a sense of memorability and worth. In other words, package yourself to win!

The results of packaging can sometimes be startling. In fact, there isn't a lawyer today worth her salt who doesn't advise her client to look good in court. "Put on your best suit, cut your straggly hair, shave the stubble" are common bits of advice. Why? Because it has been proven that the better a defendant looks in court, the lighter the sentence he or she will get. Now, you may be thinking this isn't fair; it isn't just. You're right, it isn't—but it is true. Although most of us have been taught that we should not judge a book by its cover, that is, in fact, exactly what we do, every single day of our lives, and we just can't help it.

That's right, be we jury, client, or consumer, we all are swayed by good looks. We believe if it looks good, chances are it is good. Looking good is the first step.

Most women seem to be innately attentive to their appearance. Even as children, girls tend to focus a great deal of attention on the clothes they wear and how to fix their hair. Most boys wait until adolescence before they take any notice at all of their grooming and appearance. Women generally have a greater awareness of their appearance and are more experienced in trying to capitalize on their physical attributes to make a positive impression. Additionally, women have far greater experience being judged by their appearance than men.

That's why, as far back as Cleopatra and Jezebel, women, to paraphrase Ezekiel, "paintedst" their eyes and "deckedst" themselves with ornaments. Whether it was henna for dying the fingernails, hair, and skin, kohl for lining the eyes, barley flour and butter to fight zits, or psilotum to remove unwanted hair, attention to appearance has always played an important role for women throughout history.

Now, there are exceptions to every rule, and I guess the queen of England is one. Among her other faux pas, she is known to wear a housedress with her crown. As Joan Rivers chides: If you own Scotland, England, and Wales, for God's sake at least shave your legs.

Appearance contributes greatly to your validity and to people's assessment of you in terms of your:

- Social standing
- Economic status
- Authority
- Control
- Power

- Likability
- Intelligence
- Credibility

Your appearance creates an image, that image creates a perception of you, and that perception often determines others' attitudes toward working with you. That is why people are more likely to respond to orders from someone in uniform (authority), are more likely to try to borrow a dollar from a stranger in a suit than one dressed as a bum (economic status), are more likely to think that people with glasses have the right answer (intelligence), are more likely to approach someone with a nice smile than someone with a frown (likability), are more ready to listen to the business advice of someone wearing a homburg than someone donning a beanie with a whirligig on top (credibility), and so on.

Depending on what you are selling, a more bizarre attention-getting attire may be appropriate (for example: selling T-shirts or popcorn at the beach). However, no matter what you are selling, when the buyer has choice as to whom to buy it from, appearances definitely enters into the picture. Pure and simple, the vast majority of people feel a heightened sense of confidence, no matter what they are buying, if they buy it from a person who cares about, and pays attention to, how she looks. (Most would sooner buy a hot dog from the clean-cut guy than from the slob with mustard on his beard.) Clearly you would be hard-pressed to find a customer who would feel more confident and secure in buying a high-ticket item like a computer, car, jewelry, furniture, or the like from a woman wearing her underwear over her clothes (Madonna style) than from the one wearing a neat, tasteful outfit.

Now, when we discuss "lookin' good" in the business world, I don't necessarily mean Gucci, Pucci, Armani, and Fendi. I do mean that thought, coordination, and planning when it comes to you and your wardrobe have to be part of your sales success game plan. It is not vanity; it is creating validity.

Unfortunately, when it comes to planning and thinking it through, as far as wardrobe is concerned, women have it definitely tougher than men. Men have about four pairs of shoes, two of which are totally unsuitable for work. Women have fifteen to twenty pairs of shoes, all of which can be worn to work (with pain).

Men have two belts, one black, one brown. Women have twenty belts at least, as well as scarfs, assorted jewelry, colored panty hose to coordinate, and a matching purse to load. Then we have to remember which shoulder pads Velcro into which outfit, and secure them so they don't shift. (I am currently considering implants to save time.)

In light of the choices and difficulties that we women have to deal with, the following wardrobe and grooming tips have worked well for me and will help you on your way to achieving maximum face validity with minimum hassle:

• To save both time and money, choose one basic color theme around which to build your wardrobe. For me, black works well (it hides stains better). When I first started out, I bought three good basic black *lined* skirts (never mess with slips), two pairs of good black heels, one good black bag and briefcase. I then purchased five jackets to go with black. I opted for jackets that could be worn without a blouse. This made packing, and thinking about what to wear every day, a very simple task. I have a sales colleague, Brenda, who even went further than this. Her *entire* business wardrobe is made up of only three colors: red, black, and white. It has even become her trademark or logo of sorts.

• No matter how fabulous a pair of shoes is, the first and foremost priority must be comfort. Except for telemarketing, selling is not a desk job, so you'd better take care of what moves ya. Orthodics is the latest for anyone who works on her feet. After a podiatrist's examination, if appropriate, the doctor will make a cast of your feet and fit you with a device that looks something like the innersole of your shoe. When you put this device in the shoes you are currently wearing, it really makes a difference. Poor standing habits and minor foot problems practically disappear. Teachers, lawyers, actors, clerks, etc., rave about the benefits—so do I. Orthodics runs about three hundred dollars a pair and can be the best money you have ever spent, if you stand for more than 50 percent of your day. In many cases a simple pair of over-the-counter innersoles can act as a shock absorber and will do the trick.

One last point on shoes. Believe it or not, people spend more time looking down than up. Therefore, cheap, worn, or scuffed shoes can ruin the image created by a smart suit, really fast!

- Invest in a good haircut and keep it up! Long, short, mid-length, it doesn't matter—but if you want to look more mature, go for the shorter cut. What really matters, however, is neatness, shine, color, and manageability. Common sense dictates that you avoid a look that is too bizarre, too trendy, or too outdated. If you get your hair colored, you have a commitment to keep it up every six to eight weeks, and ask your hairdresser about the new products that really make your hair shine.

- Since so many of us naturally gesticulate as we talk, in sales, hand and nail care is very important. No matter what you may think, long nails have no place in sales. Not only are they an encumbrance, but they are a distraction. If you are a nail biter, you will have to invest in sculptured nails, at least until you can kick the habit. Short to mid-length nails, freshly and simply polished, work—forget the palm trees, gold stud, or airbrushed abstract patterns.

- Makeup, if applied properly, does enhance every woman's looks. (Aren't you amazed at the before-and-after makeovers?) There are a number of good places that will start you out right with a makeover and a few good products. The big rule here is: "Less is more." If in doubt, don't use it. I always carry a colorless powder with me for shine control.

- To look at ease with yourself, and less encumbered when you enter an office, plan on carrying either a purse *or* a briefcase, not both. Make sure, if you carry a briefcase, that you hold it in your *left* hand to leave your right hand free for handshakes. When attending a business cocktail party or social function, don't carry a briefcase, and if at all possible, don't even carry a purse around with you. Leave it in your car trunk or find somewhere safe to stow it. You will feel much more at ease in "working the room" without that extra appendage. Stick a few business cards in your suit jacket pocket.

- Accessories are a pain in the neck. And dresses or suits that need belts or scarfs result in just one more thing to misplace. I highly recommend spending your accessory money on two pairs of very good gold or silver earrings and a good businesslike watch. Swaying earrings, shifting scarfs, jingling bracelets, and dangling necklaces can be distracting in a sales situation, and we want to keep the attention focused where it counts.

- Make sure your clothes fit comfortably and are tailored properly. The best Chanel suit, if it doesn't fit right, is a downright waste of money. Finding a good and quick seamstress is important.

- Personal shoppers were at one time just for the rich and famous. But now they are for everyone. The top department stores provide this service free, and the advantages to you are (1) time savings, (2) help in creating a finished look, and (3) professional advice from someone who has the experience to help you avoid making costly mistakes and who is familiar with your style, taste, and body type.

- Developing your own taste, however, is important, too. So as you look in magazines or catalogs that come your way, cut out photos or pictures of the clothes you like, and keep them in an envelope. (Remember when they announce that they are wearing it in Paris, it really means that they are wearing it nowhere else on the face of the earth.) When you meet with your personal shopper, show her the pictures you have collected, as it will more easily get across the type of clothes you like. Then she will be able to advise you as to variations on that look that would work for you.

- There are many different styles of dress that can be acceptable for business today. Keeping within these guidelines, you can lean toward the more bohemian, tweedy, classic, and even a slightly "funky" look. When done with good taste and sensibility, they work, and help you project your unique persona and style. However, at all costs, avoid looking "cute." Bows, ruffles, frills, and the like will deter your face validity in the business world. Also, stay away from dressing like one of the boys—keep the ties at home for sportswear. Try to present the image of looking rich without looking gaudy.

- Create an "emergency five-to-ten-pound-spread" section of your closet. By that, I mean *always* have two different outfits ready that you feel good in and that look good on you even if your weight fluctuates a few pounds.

- Since smiling is essential in selling, you must make absolutely certain that your smile looks great. Today, with the advent of "bonding," dentists can perform miracles, and the chipped front tooth that has caused you to cover your mouth when you smile for the past ten years can be fixed in ten minutes.

- Anticipation can save embarrassment and anxiety, so practice preventive grooming. Keep an extra pair of panty hose hidden in the zipper compartment of your purse or attaché case, and have a few safety pins available for an emergency. I also recommend keeping an extra pair of shoes in your car, since hobbling into a meeting with one heel broken off makes it hard to fake class. Clear nail polish for stocking runs, a nail file, and breath spray (not mints) are also necessities. When I travel I always bring a small bottle of nail polish in the color I have on for touch-ups. Don't bother changing nail colors to match your outfits; stick with a color that will go with all your outfits.

- Next time you travel, use the packing tip that I learned from a flight attendant. Fold your clothes by placing a garment with its top lying against one edge of the suitcase; the bottom half of the garment hangs out over the side of the suitcase. Place as many items as you are taking in the suitcase, piling them up with all the ends hanging out. (Place long items horizontally, short items vertically.) After everything is in place, flip the ends up into the suitcase. You will end up with each garment padding another at a crucial fold line.

- Fitting in with your customer's image and style can create an unconscious link and expedite the initial acceptance process. Therefore, be smart and *scope out the company you'll be making a sales call to beforehand.* Notice what the top management is wearing and make sure that you have something in your wardrobe that seems to fit in. If the company seems to favor the more formal look of a tailored business suit—get yourself one. If the company is more casual, be neat, but dress down to fit in. In case of doubt, always project the more formal rather than casual look.

- Looking good, creating positive face validity, goes beyond your physical appearance. In fact, anything the client sees must look good, because caring about yourself and your environment equates to a client as caring about your work, product, and service. Your briefcase must be neat, your desk must appear uncluttered and organized, and your car can't look like a big purse on wheels. In fact, in sales your car should be equipped just like your office: Pen, pencils, Rolodex, tape, scissors, and a tape recorder should always be with you. By the way, a high-quality briefcase and pen are noticeable assets.

Looking good takes time, effort, and money, but most of all, it takes thought. You've got to do more than just pay attention to your appearance; you must become aware of the effect and impact your appearance will have on others.

Understanding the importance of looking good and what it means in starting the sales process off on the right foot is essential. Since women have been programmed since childhood to be conscious of our appearance, and since we have had a great deal of experience manipulating our appearance (to appeal to both other women and men)—*don't stop now.* In the field of sales it will pay you back in more than compliments.

CREATING THE BUYING FRAME OF MIND

□ □ □

REASON #5
Women Make People Feel Good

Women are natural confidence builders; they enjoy giving compliments and praise and know how to show their "love." These acts make people feel good, confident, and positive. Those feelings enhance the buying frame of mind.

Though shoppers may hit the half-off lingerie table, the sale dress rack, the three-cans-of-motor-oil-for-a-dollar shelf, the warped wood aisle, or the reduced-price costume jewelry bins to cheer themselves up when they are feeling down, those who study the buying habits of today's consumers have discovered that most people make major purchase decisions when they feel good, not bad. Therefore, unless you are bent on or relegated to spending your entire sales career at the "Incidentals—reduced for quick sale" counter, it makes good sense and profitable sales practice to understand that part of your job as a salesperson requires an ability to make your customer feel good.

Quite simply, most people are not inclined to trust their judgment when they feel "off": bad, unsure, or down. They may not recognize this consciously and may in fact even make a purchase decision when not feeling up to par. However, many of those items purchased under that frame of mind get returned or fail to live up to the buyer's unrealistic expectations. On the other hand, items purchased during a buyer's good frame of mind are bought with more confidence and a clearer head, and therefore have a better and more realistic chance of satisfying. This is a crucial sales concept that few salespeople understand and even fewer exploit.

There are four major ways to make people feel good—which can easily be incorporated into the "warm-up" aspect of your sales presentation. Fortunately, women excel in all four of them.

1. Bolstering confidence
2. Using flattery
3. Making people feel important
4. Demonstrating "love"

BOLSTERING CONFIDENCE

The last time I bought a car, I expected the usual harrowing experience and runaround. You see, in all my years, I had never walked out of any car showroom happy. Oh, I'd drive to the showrooms happy, I'd enter happy, but for some reason, I would usually leave with knots in my stomach, a lump in my throat, and tears in my eyes. This time was different. Here's what happened:

I parked my rusty yellow Datsun and entered the showroom. A saleswoman stood up from one of those desks that are strategically positioned by the window, extended her hand in that warm professional sales style, introduced herself, welcomed me to the dealership, and requested my name, in what seemed to be one all too smooth and easy maneuver. "Boy, she is good," I thought. "I'd better watch out for her." I reluctantly provided my name and defensively waited for her next move. Then, sure enough, with what sounded like the beginning of the typical car salesperson's attempt to gain the upper hand, the dialogue started:

SHE: "Did I see you drive up in that yellow Datsun?"
ME: "Yes, that was me."
SHE: "Is that *your* Datsun?"

ME: "Sure is."

SHE: "Thinking of trading that in?"

ME: "I might."

Then I waited. I knew it was going to come. Her next words were going to be typical of all other car salespeople I have encountered. The line would go: "Bet you can't wait to get rid of that hunk of junk!"

But that's *not* what happened here. You could have knocked me over with a feather when she said, "Nice car. Bet you've had fun driving it. I always liked that year Datsun. That's a good car."

My first reaction was one of relief. Thank you, Lord, for letting me find the most inexperienced, stupid car salesperson on the face of the earth.

My next reaction was disbelief. Does this woman actually think that she is going to sell me a new car by telling me how good my old car was? Boy, is this lady dumb. (She probably flunked out of sales training.) Is this lady crazy?

Dumb? Hardly. Crazy? Like a fox. This woman knew what she was doing. She understood a vitally important element of selling. She knew that the best way to get me to make a new decision, another decision, was to make me feel good about my past decisions. In essence, she was pointing out to me that I had made a great decision once, and I could do it again. She was not tearing me down, she was pumping me up. She was certainly not convincing me to keep the Datsun. She was convincing me that I had good decision-making ability and that I was going to exercise that ability again, right there, in that showroom, with her, that day—and I did.

This salesperson was a master at bolstering my buying confidence. I was not surprised that she was a woman.

As part of the nurturing instinct, women build up the confidence of their children ("Try out for the soccer team, you're good enough to make it"). They build up the confidence of their men ("You deserve that promotion; you have a right to go in there and ask for it"). They build up the confidence of their friends ("I always told you, you were too good for him—you can do much better"). There is no doubt that if I want my morale boosted, or my confidence enhanced, I seek out my girlfriends. Yes, women are well practiced and good at it.

USING FLATTERY

Whoever said that flattery will get you nowhere? Boy, were they wrong. Flattery will get you everywhere, but you have to know how to use it.

When my business was just starting out, I realized the importance of packaging my reports to look professional. But I couldn't afford to buy desktop publishing or take my written work to a printer. I had read about a labeling machine that would enable me to produce lines of type for proposal headings. It promised an "affordable professional printing look" in the comfort of my own office. I called the company and a salesman came right over. He brought one of these portable labeling machines with him to give me a firsthand demonstration.

The machine probably wasn't too difficult to operate, since it took him only a few minutes to cover the procedure. However, since I am known to be mechanically "declined," I repeatedly expressed my concern. My salesman reviewed the instructions twice more but went on to stress that I couldn't be that mechanically deficient if I was able to use the complicated phone system he saw on my desk, or the state-of-the-art copier he noted in the back room.

As he was setting up his machine for a demonstration, he complimented me on understanding the value of sending out a professional-looking product. He added that I appeared more savvy than many of his clients whom he had to first convince of the importance of this marketing step.

Then, seated at my side, he patiently taught me step by step how to print out my name. As the hour progressed, and as I became more proficient in printing out "Nicki Joy," this salesman kept repeating phrases such as "You sure catch on fast," "This is great," "You're very quick," "You are using this like a pro." And I, seeing my name spilling out in print all over the floor, kept thinking, "God I'm good!!"

Needless to say, I bought the machine. I did use it and it did help in presenting my work. But what really put me in the frame of mind to *buy* right then and there was the flattery and praise that salesman gave me.

Flattery and praise make people feel good, reassure them, and enhance their self-esteem. Women, as natural givers of praise and flattery, have another edge when it comes to sales by bringing this propensity into the sales arena.

Even though the example I used was a salesman, I bet he was a rarity, as I find that women are much more adept at and comfortable using flattery and praise than men. In fact, sometimes I think that men go out of their way to ignore opportunities to flatter. I even think they go so far as to use those opportunities to do the opposite.

Just recently I was in a hardware store working with a salesman. All of a sudden one of his long-lost buddies walked in. "Fred, you old potbellied, beer-drinking, balding fool. How the hell are you?" Fred laughed and all seemed simpatico. For a moment there I tried to imagine if two women could get away with this deliberately unflattering greeting. There I would be working in the office and the door would open. "Hey, Doris, you bleached-blond, water-retaining whale. How the hell are you?" No, it would never work. Doris would leave immediately, no doubt in tears, and I would probably have to check myself into the Institute for the Severely Insensitive.

Be it sensitivity, be it verbiage, be it socialization, be it style, women are more prone to give praise than ridicule, and should bring that aspect of their personas into the business of sales. By doing so, they will make their customers feel good and put them in a buying frame of mind.

By praise and flattery, I am not suggesting that you use false praise. People are astute today and they can usually tell whether you genuinely like their jacket, concept, briefcase, idea, or hairstyle. You should never say, "I love those earrings" if they remind you of hubcaps. You should never comment, "Gee, those black socks look great with those puce

Bermuda shorts" if the fashion police should be notified for
the offense. And please refrain from cooing, "Oh, your baby
is darling" if it looks like a sniveling miniature Mexican Chi-
huahua.

However, if you do sincerely like something about your
customer, now is not the time to hold your tongue. Just don't
overdo it. But remember that flattery and praise don't have
to be directed toward something personal, like appearance
or possessions. Flattery and praise can come in many forms.
Some sales flattery and praise phrases that work well:

"You seem to really know what you are looking for."

"I can tell you know what you are talking about."

"Not everyone can understand this as easily as you do."

"Your experience in this field is obvious."

"You seem to have very high standards."

"I can tell that you appreciate quality."

"You have really done your homework; you sure know
   what's out there."

Flattery and praise are powerful. One of my business jour-
nals recounted that a psychology professor, studying the effect of flattery and praise, sent cards to approximately one
dozen acquaintances whom he selected randomly. Each card
had the same message, "Congratulations, you should be very
proud."

The result of his little experiment was quite interesting.
Each of the people who received a card replied with a hearty
thank-you. They reported new promotions, new home purchases, new grandchildren, victories in sports or school.
Some were pleasantly surprised by this professor's acknowledgment, but all felt that they indeed had something to be
praised about . . . congratulated for. So what's the point? The
point is that everybody wants praise, it is relatively easy to
give out, and there is usually something in everyone that you
can indeed find to extol.

MAKING PEOPLE FEEL IMPORTANT

Something happened on the home front that brought to light a really interesting sales point. My husband, Steve, was sitting on the couch with his pet remote control, flipping through the channels. I was sitting next to him, and as usual, was getting engrossed in each channel seconds before he decided to change it. The doorbell rang. Steve turned his head toward the door, looked back to me, and said, "Nicki, it's a kid. Probably selling magazines or candy bars. You're in sales. If anyone can get rid of him quickly, you can."

"Sure," I said, "After all, you have worked so hard today playing tennis and taking out the garbage that you shouldn't have to budge from that sofa."

As I opened the front door, it appeared that Steve's assessment made through the sheer curtains had proved correct. There stood a young boy about nine years old selling magazines. He wasn't neat about it, as the information in booklet form was trailing along behind him. He was cute, though, and had one of those baseball caps on backward (beak-in-back/hole-in-front arrangement). Needless to say, I wasn't buying. I currently had two years worth of *Time* magazines to get through and was still reading *Harper's Bazaar* from 1989 to catch up on the fashion trends. The last thing I needed was another magazine in the house.

The kid saw me start to shake my head no before he got out his first word. So I don't know if he altered his pitch accordingly, but gee, was it interesting.

BOY: "Is this 34 Tanterra Circle?"

ME: "Yes, it is."

BOY: "Is this the Joy residence?"

ME: "Yes, it is."

BOY: "Are you Nicki Joy?"

ME: "Yes, I am, but—"

BOY: "Are you *the* Nicki Joy?"

OUTCOME: Subscriptions to *Field & Stream, Jack and Jill, Boxing USA,* and *Modern Farmer.*

What happened here? To cut to the quick, the kid made me feel good. The kid made me feel important. And no one, including yours truly, is immune to this. People respond to people who make them feel worthwhile and give them recognition. It has been said that six-eighths of the world goes to bed hungry every night, but that seven-eighths of the world goes to bed hungry for recognition.

Women seem to innately understand the benefits of making people feel important, and, in fact, seem to like to do it. Women do not see making other people feel important as a threat to their own position. To a date: "You pump gas for a living? How interesting!" To a child: "You will always be Mommy's big boy." To a friend: "I need your advice."

Now, it may seem that in the sales area, making your customers or clients feel important would be too difficult a task to execute. After all, you would have to know about them, research their background, and understand their achievements, accomplishments, and strong suits. Well, there are ways of making people feel a sense of importance without having access to their personnel dossiers.

The first way you let people know they are important to you is through the simple act of acknowledging them immediately as they enter your sales environment. It seems so very basic to acknowledge someone who enters your office or store, but it is amazing how many people do not realize the significance of this little bit of business.

Recently Steve and I decided to celebrate our twenty-ninth anniversary by treating ourselves to a special gourmet French dinner. (Twenty-five years, as you may know, is "silver"; twenty-nine, they don't tell you, is "shrapnel.") In any event, we made reservations at one of those pricey places with "Chez" in its name. Entering through the front door, we approached the maitre d's podium to find no one manning the post. We stood around for quite a while as waiters zipped past us with their food undercover and their noses in the air. This went on for almost fifteen minutes with no one even seeming to notice or care that we had indeed arrived. After about the twenty-minute mark, Steve and I left. What miffed us was not that everyone employed at this restaurant was so busy, it was that no one, not one single person, acknowledged us.

All they had to do was recognize our arrival and we would have gladly sat at the bar to wait, probably even well past our dinner reservation hour. We felt unimportant to these people, and feeling good that night was important to us.

Though the act of acknowledgment, especially during the initial meeting-and-greeting process, can make or break a sale, making your clients feel important doesn't end here. There are several ways, during the course of your presentation, to get across to them that they are important to you. The obvious has been used in sales scenarios for years. It involves simply telling the customer outright, "Your business is important to us." But there are other less obvious ways to get the message across, ways that create a good feeling, a feeling of customer importance that will set them in the buying frame of mind.

Here are some sales phrases that convey to your customer his or her importance to you:

"Ms. Jones, your feedback is what we are looking for here."

"Mr. Smith, your input in designing this system is absolutely necessary to help make it work right."

"You work for a fine company, and I have heard that they are very selective in hiring."

"Based on your experience, how would you say we stack up against the competition?"

DEMONSTRATING "LOVE"

Another principle related to the business of life that has proven to be very effective when applied in the sales world has to do with the premise that *we like people who like us.* This is not a complicated concept, but one that is especially critical in a competitive marketplace.

Have you ever bought from someone you didn't like? Sure

you have. But I bet if you had a choice, if someone you did like was selling a similar product at a similar price, you would buy from that person. In other words, if competition doesn't exist, the customer with a need does not have to like you to buy from you. However, when competition abounds, as it does in most areas, you'd better know how to get them to like you. Even the *Harvard Business Review* talks about relationship selling and how important it is in today's world to hone those skills that create likability. But did you know that one of the quickest routes to get people to like you is to show that you like them? It works like a charm.

We had some "friends" with whom we used to go out with on a somewhat regular basis. Lord knows why, because they wouldn't even be our first choice if our third choice was busy, but they were quite assertive in pursuing our friendship and in making the movie or dinner plans that we would somehow fall into. Steve and I always felt roped into it, but we would continually wind up agreeing to spend our free evenings with them. We didn't like these people, we just kept going out with them. Why? Because they liked us soooo much. They constantly told us how much they cared about us, how they loved to be with us, and that we were their "best friends." It is strange, but their "like" for us was very powerful. It effected a certain hold on us. No matter how hard we tried, we kept on rationalizing that they couldn't be so bad if they liked us so much.

The fact is that we do tend to like people who like us, often just because they like us. That "like factor" certainly acts as a magnet. Now, granted, to create genuine loyalty with friends or business associates, you need to do more than just demonstrate that you like them, but if they know that you do like them, it certainly keeps your foot in the door longer. It certainly gives you an edge that makes them feel inclined to deal with you.

One way to show people you like them is to spend time with them or be willing to spend time with them. Interestingly enough, we all know that time is a very precious commodity in our lives today. In fact, it has been said that the one thing we all have less of than disposable income is disposable time.

The new breed of economists concur that today's monetary unit is no longer the dollar; it has become the second. I know also that the recession has shrunk not only the dollar, but time as well, for I remember saying, "Wait a minute"; then it became "Wait a second." Now I say, "wait a sec."

Because time is so very valuable today, the gift of giving it has become correlated with "love." Quite frankly, if you feel that someone doesn't love you, dollars to doughnuts, I'll bet you feel that the person is not spending enough time with you. Yes, giving one's time has become one way to demonstrate love, like, interest, and caring.

We have recognized this as a society, perhaps on an unconscious level, and have copped out with the phrase "quality time," which has come to mean "not a hell of a lot of time, but good, intense, one-on-one time." Perhaps the quality time concept is used to justify lack of "quantity time." But all I know is that in life, as in sales, showing people that you are interested in and willing to spend time with them, presenting people with the elusive and very desirable gift of time, transmits a positive message that you like them. And liking them attracts them to you. However, a note of caution. Be careful not to carry this to an extreme as you never want to appear desperate for business.

Women, again, with their naturally more demonstrative style will find it easy to verbalize their like for someone else and to demonstrate "love." Additionally, women seem to better understand, and more readily see the need to act upon, the time/love equation. During my twenty-plus years in business, the women I have met have expressed a stronger feeling of responsibility to spend time with their children, loved ones, and ailing relatives than have the men. Maybe this is because women's traditional role required this; nevertheless, women have gained a clear sense of the time/love correlation.

Therefore, let us take a look at some sales phrases that women will have no trouble using and that will serve to show their prospects their like for them. And remember, they must like you and trust you before they really listen to and absorb anything you say. Phrases like:

"I love this business because I get a chance to meet with people like you."

"I feel very comfortable working out the details with you."

"I have really enjoyed this opportunity to talk to you and look forward to the next time that we can get together."

In sales, building up your prospects' confidence, using flattery, making them feel important, and letting them know that you like them can pay you back in megabucks. People make major decisions and spend money when they feel good. They buy when they feel confident in themselves, confident in their decision-making abilities, and when they're in a positive frame of mind. Remember, the higher-priced the item, the more this principle applies. But no matter what you may be selling, these four powerful means of creating a positive buying frame of mind are some of the simple things great sales are made of.

– 6 –
ASKING IS THE ANSWER

□ □ □

REASON #6
Women Are Naturally Inquisitive

Since we sell to the people we know most about, selling is not telling—it is asking. Women are comfortable asking, and extremely experienced at it. Don't you think?

T he easiest people to sell to are the people who can't buy. They're terrific! They'll listen attentively to your entire presentation. They'll gladly give you their input, feedback, and time. They'll get involved, nod their heads in agreement, raise objections, and let you answer those objections. They'll be able to take delivery immediately, and probably have enough room in their warehouse at this very moment to hold four years worth of your stock.

Just when you think you have died and gone to heaven, you find out that all you really have done was die. Just when you think you have been dealt a winning poker hand, you realize your customer has been playing "go fish." Your customer told you everything you wanted to hear—except the one thing you needed to know. Does she make the decision to buy? Your customer told you everything you wanted to hear—except the one thing you forgot to ask. Can she afford your product?

We make sales to the people we know most about, so you'd better learn how to find out about your prospect. In order to know people, you have to be able to ask. The operative word here is "ask," and asking is qualifying.

Qualifying, learning about your prospect—everything from her buying needs to her capabilities—really knowing her, is so important that salespeople have been trying for years to figure out ways to do it quickly, thoroughly, and painlessly.

I'll never forget the quick qualifying scheme that one new home salesperson suggested to avoid having to ask questions to learn about his customers. His idea was to set up a series of doors, designed to help him qualify the customer. When a customer pulled into the parking lot, arrows would direct him to an adjacent building with three doors—one door marked RANCH home, the second door marked SPLIT LEVEL, and the third door marked TWO-STORY COLONIAL. After selecting the appropriate door, the customer would move on to a second series of doors. One marked THREE BEDROOMS, the other marked FOUR BEDROOMS, and the third marked FIVE BEDROOMS. After walking through the appropriate door, the customer would come to a third set of doors . . . ONE BATH, TWO BATHS, THREE BATHS. Upon selecting the door of his choice in that category, he would be confronted by yet another two doors. Over door A the sign would read INCOME *UNDER* $35,000, while over door B it would read, INCOME *OVER* $35,000. If the customer entered door A, he would then find himself back in the parking lot.

Qualifying, an essential in sales, can cause anxiety among even the most seasoned salespeople, because on the surface it seems to involve prying and a high level of assertiveness. But *once women capitalize on their innate ability to ask even the most sensitive questions with confidence and tact, qualifying buyers becomes a breeze and doesn't require tricks or gimmicks.* Qualifying involves asking questions to uncover the customer's complete buying situation in terms of:

- Needs
- Wants
- Time frame
- Buying readiness
- Motivation
- Experience
- Current status

- Decision-making power
- Financial viability

Yes, qualifying involves asking questions. To put it succinctly, it requires: **Properly Posing Probes to the Prospects to Pinpoint their Power, Past, Pocketbook, Priorities, and Preferences, so that we can Predetermine the Proper Product and Present it Positively.**

Women are comfortable asking questions and are even encouraged to do it from a young age. Remember when you were learning about boys? What was the advice you read in *Seventeen* magazine? "Ask him about himself," they told you. "Draw him out." ("A cell biologist, huh? What exactly does that involve?" "Oh, I never met a man with such an extensive beer can collection before. How interesting! Do you remember enough to tell me how you got started?")

Research also indicates that women's tendency to ask questions can stem from their feeling of responsibility to keep a conversational flow going. How many times have you been at a party and felt the need to jump in to keep the conversation alive? Even when it wasn't your party! Men don't do this.

Men are also much less likely to ask personal questions. They figure that personal information will come out when and if the speaker wishes to divulge it. Men equate asking with prying.

Bob to Fred

BOB: "So, good buddy, where you been?"

FRED: "Oh, around."

BOB: "What's up?"

FRED: "Not much."

BOB: "Same old thing, huh?"

FRED: "Yep, but I'm moving back to Arizona 'cause Carol and I got divorced last month."

BOB: "Oh? . . . Hope it all works out. Hey, did you catch the last Redskins game? I mean, those guys can really move that ball, can't they?"

Women, in contrast, equate asking with interest and caring. To women, inquiry shows interest, and interest keeps people talking. Women understand the subtle difference between probing and prying. People who pry are usually only superficially interested in the information. Their goal is to satisfy their curiosity or own self-serving purpose. Probing, on the other hand, requires the same thoroughness as any diagnostic process and is exploratory in nature, but the information gleaned is used to benefit both parties. *Asking personal questions that encourage an open response comes easily to women.*

The scene: a crowded bus. Two women seated side by side.

WOMAN #1:   "A letter from your boyfriend, huh?"

WOMAN #2:   "Yeah, I don't think he is coming back."

WOMAN #1:   "You're kidding. Why not?"

WOMAN #2:   "He met another woman in Rome and took her to Paris."

WOMAN #1:   "Did you think you were going to get married?"

WOMAN #2:   "Absolutely. I mean, the ring, the condo, everything. Wouldn't you?"

WOMAN #1:   "Sure. Will you speak to him again?"

WOMAN #2:   "You bet, he's calling tonight."

WOMAN #1:   "You have got to update me on this. I want to know everything he says. I am here for you, whatever you need. Give me a call tomorrow. Don't forget, OK?"

WOMAN #2:   "Sure, thanks for being so interested and for caring. By the way, what did you say your name was?"

Novice saleswomen who don't understand the importance of early up-front qualifying often fail to use their natural asking and probing skills to learn about their customers. They assume customer viability or they allow customers to qualify themselves. This modus operandi usually turns out to be a monumental waste of time. Since time is definitely money in sales, it's essential to know *as soon as possible* if your customer is indeed viable. As Kenny Rogers once said, "You've gotta know when to hold 'em, know when to fold 'em." And in the field of sales, it is up to you to determine just that.

Before any direct selling can take place, you must assess needs. You cannot rely on the customers to reveal, of their own accord, the key information you need to truly understand what they are looking for and how you can help them. The inclination may be for you to think that customers today are pretty smart and they know what to ask. Some salespeople believe this premise so much that their entire presentation centers around "Do you have any questions?" or "What questions can I answer for you?"

Today's consumers may be the smartest, sharpest, and most sophisticated of all time, but don't let that convince you to rely on them to ask all the questions: They still don't know all the right questions to ask.

Every day I encounter intelligent people in all walks of life who ask the wrong questions. In writing this I have to laugh thinking of a recent incident that happened to me at a local shopping mall. After several hours of heavy-duty shopping, I returned to my car to realize that I had locked my keys inside. Sensing my frustration, a gentleman parked nearby, who I later learned was a mechanical engineer, walked over and said, "Whoa, what happened here?" I said, "I locked my keys in the car." "Wow, how did you do that?" he asked. I wanted to respond, "It wasn't easy. I had to creep out of the exhaust pipe!"

Good salesmanship requires knowing the right questions even more than knowing the right answers. The majority of people who don't make it in sales don't make it, in fact, because they don't know the importance of finding out what their customers do know. The majority of people who don't make it in sales don't make it because they don't know how to ask the right questions. Many of these salespeople may have incredible product knowledge and have developed a comprehensive, fact-filled presentation. The problem is that they become product spokespeople rather than salespeople.

I have found that being a product spokesperson is an easy trap for a man to fall into. Traditionally, men enjoy being in a position that allows them to exhibit their knowledge, show their expertise, and maintain center stage. Effective asking requires a careful blend of key comments or points about your product or service mixed with well-planned questions that are nonthreatening but formulated to encourage a free-flowing response. Women, because of their propensity for and comfort in asking, are much less likely to develop the spokesperson pattern. Women just need to value their talent for asking questions in sales and then learn the right questions to ask.

THE VALUE OF ASKING QUESTIONS IN SALES

There are ten benefits to asking questions. Questions:

1. Make people feel important
2. Get attention
3. Elicit answers and provide information
4. Give you control
5. Enable you to best highlight your product's strengths
6. Encourage the thought process
7. Allow people to talk
8. Provide you direction
9. Show interest and caring
10. Help create the "yes" momentum

Questions Make People Feel Important

Do you feel more important when someone tells you something or asks you something? Most of us, when asked our opinion or thoughts about anything, feel a sense of importance. Therefore, a prospect who encounters a salesperson who is willing to ask and then, of course, to listen to the answer feels more respected, honored, and valued. Asking is one more way to make your prospect feel important in the sales process.

Questions Get Attention

People don't listen to what you tell them, they listen to what you ask them. It was always very easy in college to drift off to the mental Bahamas during huge lecture classes, because I knew the professor wasn't going to ask any questions of me or anyone else. But boy, my attention level really changed in those small discussion groups. I had to stay alert because I knew the format here—I was expected to participate. My input, feedback, responses, and answers were part of the lesson plan. It didn't matter whether it was because I wanted to preserve my dignity and not look stupid in front of my classmates, or whether the topic of the moment really interested me. The point is, I paid attention to what was being said. If you want to get your message across in sales, if you want to keep your prospect's attention—you'd better understand this principle.

Questions Elicit Answers and Provide Information

When we're asked a question, a trigger mechanism is set off in our minds and most of us feel compelled to respond. The act of answering a question is almost reflexive. From our early years in school, we have been conditioned to answer the question if we want to look smart. By not answering a question, we rouse feelings in others of suspicion, doubt, and even inadequacy. When a politician does not answer the question posed, we become suspicious. When a defendant in court pleads the Fifth, we assume the worst. Therefore, since most of us have been conditioned to answer questions to avoid looking bad in any way, when questions are asked, answers spill forth. And answers are what we want in sales.

In triggering the natural answering response, you can gain critical information that people don't readily volunteer. That information can help you better understand your customer's point of view and bypass some of the generalities ("I really like this house") that people tend to make—getting down more to the specifics ("The first-floor den would make a great office").

One form of questioning that you will use in sales to get information and answers is *open probes*. Open probes are questions designed to enable you to learn more about the prospect and adjust your presentation accordingly. Open probes are so named because they "open up" the prospect. Though they can be effectively used all throughout the course of a presentation, they are especially helpful in the initial stages to help you uncover what is on your prospect's mind.

Open probes are questions that elicit more than a yes/no response. They are questions that beckon elaboration and start with "Who," "What," "When," "Where," "Why," and "How."

"*How* did you hear about our company, Mr. Smith?"

"*What* are some of the key features you are looking for in a service of this type?"

"*Where* are you looking to expand your company's international marketing focus?"

Questions Give You Control

The person in life who asks the questions is the one in control. Think of a classroom scenario; the teacher can at any time point to someone and ask a question. In doing so, the teacher establishes control. In a courtroom the judge can stop the proceedings at any time and say, "I have a question." That question gets answered and that questioner, the judge, is in control. In an interview situation, it is usually the interviewer who has control.

In fact, it is interesting to note that most politicians lose control, make mistakes, and put their feet in their mouths during a press conference, not during a speech. You see, during the press conference, the press is asking the questions. The press is in control. Naturally, in sales our object is not to try to trip someone up or establish ourselves as the obvious controller, but it is important to recognize the benefits to be gained and the position you give yourself when you ask questions.

Closed probes are questions that require a simple yes or no response. They are designed to specifically help you gain and maintain the control you need during the presentation. They are questions that help you direct, lead, and steer the customer. *Closed probes are most effectively used after you have used open probes* and once you have determined which way to guide the conversation.

"Can you see how this service can eliminate some of your everyday hassle?"

"Will you be able to take delivery on Thursday?"

"Are you willing to set up a demonstration for your staff next week?"

Questions Enable You to Best Highlight Your Product's Strengths

Many buyers today don't believe what salespeople say. They figure that salespeople have to say certain things because they are trying to sell the product. This poses a difficult problem for salespeople, because they have to figure out a way to get their message—their product's strengths—across in a believable manner. Here again, asking is the answer.

Consider this interaction:

SALESPERSON: "These double-pane windows are the most energy-efficient out there."

PROSPECT'S THOUGHTS:	"He's gotta talk like this—he's trying to make me buy these windows."

Now consider rephrasing the sales statement into a question:

SALESPERSON:	"Let's take a look at these windows, because energy efficiency is important to you, isn't it?"

PROSPECT'S THOUGHTS:	"Yes, it sure is—maybe I better take a look at these windows."

I guarantee the prospect is not going to answer, "No, we don't care about energy efficiency when buying a window. We actually like to sleep with the wind blowing through our hair."

Consider this interaction:

SALESPERSON:	"You will love the people who are members of this health club—they are just like you."

PROSPECT'S THOUGHTS:	"Right. She's gotta say this kind of stuff. Anyway, how does she know what I'm like?"

Now consider rephrasing the sales statement into a question:

SALESPERSON:	"Joining a health club that has people you feel comfortable with—people like you—as members would be important to you, wouldn't it?"

PROSPECT'S THOUGHTS:	"Sure it would. I guess since she put it that way, they must have people here just like me."

I guarantee the prospect is not going to answer, "No, I want to join a club that has a bunch of idiots for members, people I can't relate to on any level."

What happens when a sales statement is rephrased into a sales question is interesting. In essence, by posing your product's strengths in question form, you are implying, suggesting, and intimating that your product or service has the qualities in question. This format eliminates natural sales resistance and encourages thought transference, which in essence, in sales, involves getting your customer to say or think the message that you want to get across.

Questions Encourage the Thought Process

Believe it or not, most people enjoy thinking. Most people actually enjoy using their brains to answer questions. There is a reason why "Wheel of Fortune" and "Jeopardy" have remained on the air for years. There is a reason why Twenty Questions maintains its popularity and Trivial Pursuit gained such a following. Yes, the fact is that when given an opportunity to think, to answer a question, most people jump at the chance. So simply capitalize on this human "quirk" when selling what you have to sell.

Questions Allow People to Talk

Most people, even introverts, prefer talking to listening. Since that is the case, people will, more readily than you may think, seize an opportunity to expound, elaborate, embellish, or enlighten. Use questions as an opportunity to allow your prospects to do exactly what they'd like to do: *talk, talk, talk*.

Questions Provide You Direction

Questioning is a two-way street. Part of the sales process *definitely* involves encouraging questions from your prospects. The interesting thing about questions is that often by questioning your prospect's questions, you will get a better handle on how to proceed and what answer to give. When I say what answer to give, I am not implying that you lie or mislead the prospect. What I am saying is that since selling is a matter of highlighting the positive and downplaying the negative, you have to first discern what your prospect would consider a positive or a negative. And believe me, some of the best salespeople get fooled by forgetting to question the question if there are multiple possible answers.

Consider this interaction:

PROSPECT: "When considering buying this home, I have to ask you if there are schools nearby."

NONQUESTIONING SALESPERSON: "Sure are; glad you brought that up. There is the elementary school, practically in your backyard. Middle school two blocks away, and a high school within walking distance."

PROSPECT: "Well, if that's the case, forget this house. Last thing I want is an elementary school in my backyard—I don't even have kids, and in my current neighborhood the youngsters wore a path through my lawn going to school every day."

See what happens when you use the questioning approach:

PROSPECT: "When considering buying this home, I have to ask if there are schools nearby."

QUESTIONING SALESPERSON: "Oh, is having a school nearby important to you? Do you have school-age children?"

PROSPECT: "I don't have any kids. I'd prefer not to live next to a school
because in my current neighborhood the youngsters wore a
path through my lawn."

At this point, the salesperson can adjust the tone of the presentation to minimize the proximity of the school to the home and to introduce new information into the conversation that may not have been emphasized otherwise, such as the walking paths used by the students in the area, the natural barrier of trees that surround the yard, etc.

Questions Show Interest and Caring

Think back to a conversation you had with someone. A conversation that felt good. A conversation that made you sense the other person was really interested and cared about what you were saying. I am willing to bet the family farm that the other person asked questions. He wanted to know more. He made you elaborate. He asked for specifics. His questions not only spurred you on, but demonstrated interest and caring in you or the topic, or both. Women, as I said earlier, equate asking and questions with showing interest and caring—therefore, women already know why asking questions is an important key to successful selling.

Questions Help Create the "Yes" Momentum

The sale should come about from a series of questions that, when answered, will surface requirements and desires, build relationships, and eventually gain a commitment. Though you want to find out what your prospect is thinking, both pro and con, the questions you pose should be geared, as much as possible, to bringing about positive responses. You see, no matter what you are selling, the customer has to be programmed or conditioned to buy it. By posing questions that bring about a "yes" answer, you are creating a positive environment and engaging in a process that creates a "yes" momentum. In fact, it has been proven that once that yes momentum takes hold during the course of your presentation, it is likely to continue when asking directly for the order or commitment. Answering "yes" almost becomes a habit. A habit that you precipitated.

Expert salespeople know that creating the yes response is one of the values gained by asking, and they clearly know how to do it.

They use *tie-downs*. Tie-downs are little phrases geared to get a yes response. They are questions that, when tagged on to the end of a sentence, encourage agreement. The interesting thing is that linguist Robin Lakoff, among others, has found that women use this form of sentence patterning more than men.

Let's look at some common tie-downs used in the world of sales:

Wouldn't it?	Don't we?
Couldn't it?	Haven't they?
Shouldn't it?	Hasn't he?
Doesn't it?	Isn't that so?
Won't it?	Isn't that true?
Aren't they?	Didn't it?
Aren't you?	Wasn't it?
Can't you?	Won't they?
Don't you agree?	Won't you?

Now let's see how a salesperson can phrase a sentence in tie-down form:

"Having an office in this location would make life easier, *wouldn't it?*"

"You have been in need of a collating machine for a long time now, *haven't you?*"

"You can see where this could save you money, *can't you?*"

"By interfacing the computer system, communication in your office will be greatly improved, *don't you agree?*"

"Lounging on the ship's deck, smelling the fresh sea air, sounds good, *doesn't it?*"

Naturally, before using a tie-down, you must know how your prospect feels or the entire concept won't work, right? For example:

SALESPERSON: "Having this automatic redial feature on your phone will make things much quicker and easier for you, won't it?"

OFFICE MANAGER: "Not in this department, it won't. We only take incoming calls. We wouldn't need that feature at all."

That's why all the other questions you pose are so important. They will help you qualify your prospect, develop a profile on your prospect; they will help you *know* your prospect. And it is just those preliminary questions that will get you in a position to pose some of the more advanced tie-down questions that will create the yes momentum.

Indisputably the question works as a hook. It is involving and has tremendous impact. This is easily evidenced by the popularity of the question in advertising today. There is no doubt about it, the exclamation point has been taken over by the question mark. "Is it the shoes?" (an ad for Nike's Air Jordans) "Does she or doesn't she?" (a well-known ad for Clairol hair coloring) "Isn't he worth it?" (an ad for Amore cat food) . . . and the list goes on. "Are you bothered by bad breath?" "Is athlete's foot ruining your life?" "Do you suffer from tired blood?" Yes, asking is powerful. It accomplishes so much and is in essence what the art of selling is all about.

THE RIGHT QUESTIONS TO ASK

I am sure you have heard the old story about the man walking through the park who encountered an attractive woman sitting on a bench. A large dog was resting on the ground beside her. Being a dog lover and looking for a way to meet this woman, he approached planning to give the dog a pat on the head. Using the opportunity to open a conversation with this woman, he turned to her and asked, "Does your dog bite?" She looked at him, smiled, and responded with a most emphatic "No!" However, the moment the gentleman placed his hand on the dog's head, the dog whipped around and took a large chunk out of his wrist. "Hey!" he screamed to the woman. "I thought you said your dog doesn't bite." "He doesn't," the woman snapped back. "That is not my dog!"

Asking questions won't do you much good or get you far unless you ask the right questions. Consider the fact that no matter what the sales situation may be, there are five answers you need to get from your prospect, and you had better be well prepared at coming up with the right questions to get these answers. Let's look at what answers you need:

1.   *Are you ready to buy?*

This asks the time frame question: Does he feel ready, able, and willing to make a purchase decision at this time? "Mr. Jones, if perchance you found the perfect wall system for your office, would you be prepared to buy it now?" (This does not mean that you would not work with a person who is not prepared to buy at this time, it just means, to help you establish priorities, you need to know his readiness.)

2.   *Do you have a need for my product or service?*

This asks a very basic question: Does she need what you are selling? Though many people will examine or look into products or services that they want and can afford, when it comes right down to buying, the lack of the need can kill the sale or justify a delay. "Although I really want this swimming pool, I really need a new car."

This is not to say that people don't buy things they don't need, because they do. However, knowing whether there is a need or want or both will help you see where you stand on the priority list, and you can then tailor your approach properly.

3. *Are you the decision maker?*

This is an obvious question that must be asked. After all, you do not want to spend extensive selling time with someone who is not in a position to make the purchase. This is not to say that you would refuse to deal with an assistant or associate or with one member of the buying party, for that person may have critical input into the buying decision and in fact be the one who influences the decision maker.

Uncovering who you are dealing with, however, will again allow you to create a presentation that is more appropriate for the person you are speaking to and in fact provide him with ways to help influence the purchaser. "Mr. Jones, will there be anyone else who must be consulted before you decide to go ahead with this purchase?"

4. *Is what I am selling within your budget range?*

There is an old sales saying, "We want to spend our sales time with the people who can buy—that is why we qualify." Yes, affordability is a basic issue. They may need it, want it, be able to make the purchase decision, and be able to put your product to good use immediately; however, if they cannot afford to buy it, you are just blowing smoke rings and passing the time. A basic question that is used to start the financial qualification ball rolling is "Mrs. Smith, is this price in line with what you were thinking?"

Today, however, you may notice that many customers you will encounter will be uncertain as to just what they can afford. Therefore, it is part of the new and expanding sales role of the salesperson to be prepared to not only determine the prospect's affordability range, but to actually place yourself in an advisory capacity, in some cases. If necessary, you may be called on to determine creative means in budgeting (remember a budget for most companies is a flexible guideline, not something etched in stone) or financial restructuring to make what you are selling more affordable to your client.

5. *Will it fit into your specific requirements?*

This is an interesting question because it makes the prospect think about important, yet not so obvious, considerations that must come into play before she can actually purchase this product. On the surface you may feel that you would want to avoid these issues, because by avoiding them, your prospects might buy even if what you're selling will not really fit their requirements. However, a good sale is one that makes the customer happy down the road. Returns or dissatisfied customers are costly, and we must remember that the sale is not made when the customer buys it; it is made when the customer uses it.

Requirements may sound the same as needs. But they are not. There is a subtle difference in that the specificity of the requirement may not naturally surface during the need-qualifying aspect of a presentation. And they really can throw you a curve later on.

I heard a story just this week of an excited salesman who had gone over his quota, selling sixteen file cabinets to a new client. Oh, she needed sixteen file cabinets and was thrilled with the purchase. But upon delivery the next day, she realized that the back room where she had planned to set up that new filing system was the wrong configuration—the office personnel couldn't open the drawers of more than two file units at a time.

With some additional probing this salesperson could have determined the space requirements and concentrated his selling efforts on a different type of unit—one that would work. In fact, he had one such workable system in his inventory that would have suited the client's requirements perfectly, but after spending two weeks with files strewn everywhere, cursing secretaries and irate file personnel, there was no way this company wanted to try again with this same salesperson.

Another example of this concept: I was in the market for a new set of good dinner dishes. I needed something that would match my decor and have extra large dinner plates and accompanying soup bowls as part of the set. I also wanted a set of china that came with matching glassware as I just love the way that looks. I found the store that carried what I wanted, bought it, and got the entire starter set as well.

Unfortunately, this purchase did not make me happy. Because I realized all too late that this was a discontinued pattern. And being the klutz that I am—I also required replacement dishes on a regular basis. So, though I expressed my needs clearly to the salesperson, and she filled those needs, my full requirements never surfaced and were not met. Though she made the sale, I never find myself thinking of her store when I have to make a recommendation.

The beginning of any relationship is a discovery process; this especially holds true in a sales relationship. Questioning not only helps you to determine your customers' ripeness, but enables you to tailor your presentation to their needs. Later on when we talk about handling objections and closing, you will find yet another plus to mastering those question/asking skills.

The greatest qualifiers know how to approach the delicate issue of asking in a manner that is comfortable for both the customer and themselves. A successful saleswoman gave me one of the easiest and best lead-in preliminary qualifying lines that taps into the interest women naturally show. "Mr. Smith, I know your time is valuable, and I am interested in helping you, so to proceed, I need some answers."

Use lead-in phrases like this, along with your innate interest in people, to uncover your customer's buying situation. This will help your buyer feel that you are going to give information as well as obtain it. And this approach indicates that you respect the customer's time, sets you up as someone who can provide help, and assumes that the answers can indeed be easily provided. All this in one carefully thought out sentence. What more can you ask?

Women's natural inquisitiveness and customer-friendly approach allow them to comfortably qualify customers while simultaneously putting them at ease and encouraging their participation. Aren't you starting to see why you, as a woman, really have an edge in sales? You bet!

– 7 –
CAN YOU LISTEN BETTER WITH PIERCED EARS?

□ □ □

REASON #7
Women Listen

Women are naturally active listeners, which encourages people to talk. In sales, you don't talk your customers into buying, you listen them into buying. Therefore, we can use our listening edge to encourage our customers to tell us what we need to know to sell to them.

I n life, talk is cheap. The same holds true in sales. Unfortunately, many people think that when they enter sales, it gives them a license to talk. In fact, that misconception may be one thing that attracts people to the field of sales to begin with.

Though in sales you are getting paid to communicate, effective communication is far from just talking; it is listening as well. But people are hardly ever trained to develop, refine, and perfect their listening skills. Yet **listening is one of the key elements that distinguishes a company spokesperson from an effective salesperson.**

A spokesperson "sells" by telling. This approach does not take into consideration the needs or requirements of the customer.

- Selling by telling basically involves offering generic product information with the hope that something said will trigger the prospect's interest level sufficiently to get him to buy it.

- Selling by telling usually results in presenting self-serving statements to the customer ("This product is the greatest"), which makes the customer feel that you are simply there to make him buy what you are selling.
- Selling by telling is usually a monologue that excludes the customer from the conversation, and usually results in a feeling of high pressure and mistrust on the buyer's part.

Any sales trainer or professional salesperson knows the truth of the matter, **it is the best listeners (*not* the best talkers) who are the best sellers.**

Why? Because good listening makes sales happen. Good listening allows you to guide the prospect to engage in the art of self-discovery, where she discovers that what you are selling is indeed just what she needs.

One of the most frequently heard criticisms about salespeople is that they don't take the time or care to listen:

"He didn't hear what I was saying."
"All she did was talk; I could hardly think."
"Wow, that salesperson was sure fast-talking."
"That guy had no idea what I was looking for."
"I couldn't get a word in edgewise."

Good listening on the part of the salesperson accomplishes many things for both parties. When the salesperson is *really* listening, the prospect:

- Is encouraged to keep talking
- Presumes that he is being understood
- Feels valued and respected
- More readily reveals needs, wants, expectations, experience, status, etc.

When the salesperson is *really* listening:

- Critical information to tailor the product to the needs of the buyer can be learned.

- Feelings that the prospect has about the product can be discerned.
- The right to offer advice on what was heard is gained.

THE WAYS WE LISTEN

We don't talk people into buying, we listen them into buying. But understand that there are *three* ways you can listen. You can listen:

1. *Passively*
2. *Actively*
3. *Selectively*

Considering the fact that you hear with your ears but listen with your mind, *passive* listening refers only to *hearing* words or sounds. It is hearing with your ears alone. Passive listening is sometimes done just to fill a void. It is distracted listening. For example, I come home from work at the end of a grueling day. I take the lettuce and tomatoes out of the fridge. As I begin to prepare the salad, I turn on the TV, only to realize after several minutes that I am listening to Fred and Wilma arguing with Betty and Barney about Bam Bam and Pebbles. I don't turn it off. I am not really listening. It is just noise, sound to keep me company.

Passive listening can happen on another level as well. It can occur when you are listening to someone whose message you have already determined not to accept. You are just pretending to listen to appear polite.

Active listening involves absorbing, digesting, and evaluating the message being heard. It is actually *listening with your mind and your eyes as well as with your ears.*

Selective listening is somewhere in between the two extremes. Though it is more active than passive in nature, it is also more self-serving. It is hearing the words but only listening for segments of the conversation that appeal to you, or that will enable you to respond, control, or maneuver the conversation course according to your agenda.

When I was truly undecided as to which candidate to vote for in the last presidential election, I actively listened to the debates. I listened for content, understanding, and feelings. I was absorbed.

But, interestingly enough, once I chose my candidate, my listening turned *selective.* You see, I found myself comfortably ignoring parts of the verbal message that did not support my views. I found myself zeroing in on only those aspects of the candidate's message with which I could easily agree.

A CLOSER LOOK AT ACTIVE LISTENING

Let's further explore *active* listening since it is such an important component of good selling.

Active listening is "involved" listening. It is being interested enough to listen for content and understanding, as well as for feelings, if applicable. It involves giving your undivided attention to the speaker and registering all that is being said. For example, I actively listen when I stop someone on the street for directions. I listen for content and understanding because I have a vested interest in everything that person is saying at that moment.

In sales you must be an active listener because you, too, have a vested interest in everything that your prospect is saying. Remember, we sell to the people we know most about. In sales, anything and everything that is important to the buyer must be important to you. Active listening will help you detect the clues that will enable you to guide the prospect to the right decision. It will enable you to better help the person buy, which is what selling is all about.

Active listening takes energy as well as discipline. It takes a willingness on your part to submerge your own opinions and concerns and give your utmost attention to your buyer. Active listening involves resisting the urge to talk.

When you actively listen by giving attention and allowing the buyer to speak, you create an atmosphere that encourages the buyer to develop her own thoughts and intensify her personal involvement with what is being said. Additionally, active listening on your part involves an almost total immersion in the message and thoughts of the buyer. That concentration and connectedness will enable you to hear and sense more than the obvious.

Active listening involves being tuned in to unspoken words, i.e., body language and other hidden messages, that enable you to determine where the buyer stands. Being an active listener helps you stay in sync with your prospect. And if customers feel that you are in sync with them, they will disclose information to you that you need to know to sell to them.

WOMEN AND LISTENING

Yes, *in sales you must be an active listener.* So does that leave women out? Let's face it, it has always been said that women love to talk. But guess what. We love to listen, too! Yes, it's true, women demonstrate better active listening skills than men, reports Laurie Schloff, a senior research consultant at The Speech Improvement Company, Brookline, Massachusetts. Much of this stems from the fact that women are basically more interested in people than men are. Women pay better attention to what the message is and how it is being delivered. They are skilled at picking up on body language cues and understand the nuances, moods, and emotional undertones of a conversation. Women demonstrate a greater ability to understand what is being said, and women possess greater auditory memory than men—all of which helps them retain the information gleaned.

Even physiologically women have an edge over men in listening, since men tend to have poorer hearing than women, especially after the age of thirty. Additionally, men are more interested than women in establishing a position of strength and status when conversing, and men perceive talking and providing information as a means of accomplishing that. Women are traditionally more comfortable being the audience—the listener.

In sales, being a good listener is one of the most attractive qualities you can have. It makes you credible, trustworthy, knowledgeable, and unique. It gives you direction, information, insight, and power. Women are good listeners! In fact, many studies have documented that men, when they need a good ear, someone to hear them out, someone to listen to their problems, will turn to a woman rather than another man.

Women have another listening advantage over men in that they **show that they are listening more obviously than men do.** Women promote conversation and demonstrate interest and respect by:

- Nodding their heads to show involvement
- Using more direct eye contact
- Interrupting conversation less
- Making little sounds of approval

The last point (making little sounds of approval) is most interesting, a factor that I believe has contributed to some serious intergender communication problems nationwide. Perhaps you may have noticed this on your own. Men tend to treat listening as a nonresponsive skill. Men remain quiet and still while listening, and when they do respond with an occasional "uh-huh," "yup," or "yes," that simply indicates that they agree with what the speaker is saying at the time. In other words, men emit listening sounds only occasionally, and when they do, they are usually meant to indicate concurrence.

Women, on the other hand, are naturally responsive listeners. They don't have to necessarily agree with the speaker or with what is being said to make little sounds. In fact, most women are constantly sending out verbal signals that beckon further conversation and demonstrate interest. Women have a tendency to say "yes" or "uh-huh," not necessarily to indicate agreement but to let the speaker know they are listening, they are interested, or they just want the person to keep on talking.

I am willing to bet that this simple difference has caused confusion in bars across the country on Friday nights. Women do not feel men are listening when they really are . . . and men think women are agreeing with them when they really aren't.

I know what this means for women in bars, but what does it mean for women in sales? It means we have another undeniable edge. It means that if women can market themselves as the proficient listeners that they are, customers will be encouraged to talk more, and in doing so, will reveal what it is they want you to tell them. You, in turn, will be able to use the information gleaned to relate your product back to the customers' needs and sell to them effectively.

How can women expand on their natural listening skills? How do they use these superior skills to make a sale? Here are seven tips that you can implement starting today to heighten your already well-defined listening ability.

Tip #1: Repetition

This first tip, I extracted from the psychiatric profession. Boy, do they have to be good listeners. I mean, that's what they get paid for, right? They show the patient they are listening by repeating what they just heard the patient say. That act not only encourages the patient to elaborate and beckons the patient to expound on the topic, but it subconsciously makes the patient think, "This person is listening to me . . . this person cares!" A common doctor/patient dialogue may sound something like this:

PATIENT: "Doctor, I feel guilty."

DOCTOR: "Guilty?"

PATIENT: "It's my mother again."

DOCTOR: "Your mother again?"

PATIENT: "Yes, it's the holidays and she wants me with her."

DOCTOR: "She wants you with her?"

PATIENT: "Yes, she wants me there. I don't have the time."

DOCTOR: "You don't have the time?"

PATIENT: "Well, maybe I could see her on Christmas day for an hour or two."

DOCTOR: "Christmas day? An hour or two?"

PATIENT: "Yes, that's what I'll do."

You leave forty-five minutes later, seventy-five dollars poorer, thinking, "Holy Guacamole, this doctor is so perceptive. What a help."

Repetition was the help. Repetition was the essence of the doctor's approach. It spurred the speaker on, but most significantly, it showed the patient that he was being listened to.

Women, use this technique to further enhance your natural listening skills. In sales the inclination is to run away with a bit of consumer information and expound on it, when in actuality we eventually learn that listening, registering, and feeding it back can reap greater results. For example:

BUYER: "I am looking for a binding system that is easier to use."

SALESPERSON: "Easier to use?"

BUYER: "Yes, the one we have now takes so much time, requires more effort than weight lifting, and gets jammed."

SALESPERSON: "Jammed?"

BUYER: "Yeah, if we have to bind twenty or more pages, the machine gets stuck."

SALESPERSON: "This binding machine here is just what you're looking for. It is a breeze to use and has an overload button that allows you to bind up to one hundred sheets at a time. That would work for you, wouldn't it?"

Though a modified form of the psychiatric technique, this approach demonstrates active listening to its fullest.

Tip #2: "Recall Feedback"

The second "show 'em you are listening" tip, I stole from Columbo. You know Columbo, that TV detective with the rumpled raincoat and the cigar, played by Peter Falk. He's good, isn't he? Boy, you know he is listening—he shows that he never misses a word. In practically every Columbo episode there comes a point when he looks at the suspect and says those few lines that make her know she's a goner. "Mrs. McGillicuddy, remember before when you said you never drink? Well, your fingerprints were all over the Jack Daniels bottle," or "Mr. Simpson, yesterday you mentioned that you could not have possibly pushed your wife off the bridge, as you have a terrible fear of heights. So how come I found your monogrammed skydiving outfit under your bed?" Both McGillicuddy and Simpson knew the jig was up. Columbo listened and brought back what he heard to his advantage, and that is exactly what you have to do in sales.

Phrases like "Remember before when you said ..." or "Earlier on you mentioned that ..." or "You expressed that you always wanted ..." or "Based on what you stated earlier ..." all serve to again demonstrate the listening, register, feedback process at work. Engaging in this will enable you to resurface customers' needs or concerns. In this way you will show that you are an astute listener, armed and able to deal with issues critical to moving forward to the point of sale.

Tip #3: Rephrasing

Rephrase the message that you hear in your own words. For example, the prospect says, "I need a filing system with easy access to the pertinent data." Salesperson: "Then getting just the information you need quickly is important. Correct?" To make this rephrasing even more powerful, you can reflect in your statement an understanding of the feelings (in this case frustration) that accompany the buyer's message. For example, "It will be so much easier on you to have everything you need at your fingertips, won't it?"

Remember that in Chapter Two we discussed the trust-relationship benefits that can be gained when the salesperson uses the customer's exact words. However, since we also discussed that overuse of the customer's words can come off as mimicking, this rephrasing technique provides an effective alternative that still has impact.

Tip #4: Lean In

When listening, shift your position and lean in a bit toward the speaker. This action indicates interest in what is being said, and quickly shows that you are willing to listen.

Tip #5: Watch Yourself

Evaluate your own mannerisms to be sure that you don't unconsciously demonstrate boredom or lack of patience. Be sure that you are not doing something inadvertently that will distract your prospects from their train of thought. Tapping your pencil, jiggling your foot, fidgeting, or looking at your watch will translate as a clear lack of listening interest.

Tip #6: Welcome Silence

Learn to welcome silence. Don't forget, when prospects are silent, they may be contemplating the information that you gave them, and enjoying the process. If you are inclined to interrupt or feel the need to fill every silent gap, you may break the spell or disengage them from the track they are on.

Tip #7: Be Genuine

Understand that supereffective active listening involves using all these tips, as appropriate. But more than that, it involves a genuine interest in the conversation so that incor-

porating these tips will not come off as manipulative or
phony.

Active listening, as you may have surmised, takes time.
Well, understanding people takes time, doesn't it? Remember, however, that active listening from the start does not
take anywhere near the time it will take if you don't listen
actively, and you have to return, establish another meeting,
reconfirm what you thought you heard, and review how your
product can satisfy the customer's needs.

Remember, as a woman you already have a jump on men
at perfecting active listening skills. Therefore, if you want to
take this a step further, if you want to motivate, convince,
persuade, sway, entice, influence, or move anyone to do anything, appreciate how these skills can enhance your ability
in sales.

One final point just for the record. I feel that there may
be a few men out there who may have already figured out
that women have these superior listening skills. Maybe they
think the holes we put in our earlobes have contributed to
this. If this is the reasoning behind the recent ear-piercing
trend among men ... ladies ... our secret is still safe.

- 8 -
DÉJÀ DOO-DOO
(OR I FEEL LIKE I'M SAYING
THE SAME OLD STUFF OVER
AND OVER)

□ □ □

REASON #8
Women Know How to Make a Point

Women know how to convey their point in a natural, sincere, and personalized manner. This, combined with those super organizational skills, enables women to easily formulate and deliver a dynamic, fresh, and individualized sales message.

When my boys, Billy and Mitch, were little, I got tired of the frequent trips we had to make to the library to look up information for their school papers. Although I took them regularly throughout the year to borrow leisure reading books, I came to dread the five-thirty Wednesday night announcement that they had a report due the next day and absolutely had to have some sort of reference material. I decided, after several such interruptions to my routine, that an investment in a good set of encyclopedias could save me time, gas, and frustration.

I knew it was fated that we would own one of these sets of reference books when, several weeks later, I opened the front door on a late Saturday afternoon to an encyclopedia salesman who had arrived quite by chance. Unfortunately, his timing was both good and bad since, although I was prepared to buy what he was selling, he had arrived just as I was rushing to get dressed to go out. Despite my rush, however, I was prepared to write a check on the spot.

The salesman, who was relatively young and very green in terms of selling, was visibly taken aback when I explained I was getting ready to leave, but would definitely like to buy a set of his books. When I invited him in, he mumbled something about having to give his presentation and took a seat on the family room couch while setting up his demonstration set and display paraphernalia. I explained again that I was in a hurry, added that I already knew his product well, and suggested I could just write him a check now.

"Mrs. Joy," he countered, "I have to go through my presentation for you. It's just the way I've gotta do it. I just can't sell you a set of books like that."

I was a little amused and quite surprised at his response, to say the least. After several minutes of back and forth about why he couldn't just take a check and why I couldn't just sit down to listen to his spiel, in frustration I called my younger son Mitch, down from upstairs. Fortifying him with a bag of Gummy Bears, I sat him down on the sofa and thereby provided the salesperson with the audience he seemed to need. Though I found this ludicrous, I headed upstairs to get dressed. Then, for the next thirty minutes, I could overhear a very organized, well-delivered sales presentation being addressed to a six-year-old, who seemed to be enjoying everything except not being able to interrupt to ask a question.

Every salesperson needs a complete sales presentation. The complete sales presentation is everything you do to interest your prospect and help him to buy what you are selling. We have already discussed several of the components and considerations when developing a complete presentation (and there is a lot more to come), but the preceding encyclopedia scenario demonstrates two presentation pitfalls that every top-notch salesperson must keep in mind:

1.   A presentation must be organized yet flexible, interesting yet memorable, informative yet relatable; in other words, planned but not canned.

2.   A presentation must take into account, and respect, the consumer's time constraints.

PLANNED NOT CANNED

To be a great salesperson, you must learn everything about your product and then you must develop and deliver a powerful sales presentation that gets your points across. A powerful sales presentation is not only one that is informative and highlights the product's value, but it is one that is attention-getting, memorable, spontaneous, and fresh. To accomplish this, a good deal of up-front planning and organization is needed so that you are so comfortable and secure with the information you have to deliver that you can concentrate on the finer points of the delivery.

Therefore, presentation development not only involves planning for all the steps you have to take from start to finish with a prospect, but it also means gathering the information you have to get across and then finding the best ways to creatively say what it is you want to say . . . so that you don't feel as if you are simply saying the same old stuff over and over and over. This is kind of like gathering together all the ingredients you have to use for dinner and then creatively figuring out what you can do with it. Women are great at this. Let's admit it, most men look at a pound of ground beef and see a hamburger. But women look at a pound of ground beef and see tacos, meat loaf, stuffed peppers, spaghetti sauce, meatballs, beef Stroganoff, chili, sloppy joes, moussaka, and steak tartar. Need I say more?

First It's Planned . . .

Over the years I have stressed to salespeople the need to first organize the product information they have gathered in an easy-to-learn and easy-to-refer-to format. All salespeople need an organized collection of information that they use for their own purposes to fully acquaint themselves with the ins and outs of their product and to prepare their presentation. Now, some companies provide their salespeople with a categorized information binder regarding the product. However, if your company does not supply you with such a tool or if you feel the need to supplement or expand on what they have given you, you will need to develop a system to organize your product information.

The best way to organize is to create lists. You will first determine the broad categories of information you need to know about relative to your product and company. Then you make lists under each of those categories, filling in the information needed. This list-making system comes easily to women. Part of our organizational skills involves making lists. Women are great at making lists for themselves (grocery lists, party guest lists, shower gift list, Christmas card lists . . . and the "list" goes on). In fact, very often women are so good at list making that they even make lists for other people (a to-do list for the husband, a clothes-to-take-to-camp list for the kids, a what-to-clean list for the housekeeper, a who-to-call list for the baby-sitter . . . and that "list" goes on, too). Well, in sales, getting your information ready for your presentation really involves just the same thing. Some examples:

Your Company

Background, history, founder, mission statement, operating philosophy, size, scope of operation, sales volume, growth, track record, awards, recognition, client list, personnel training, etc.

Service—Policies and Procedures

Warranties, guarantees, response time, repair records, registering service requests, etc.

Product Line

Prices, types, colors, sizes, features, options available, etc.

The Competition

Quality, value, pricing, usability, adaptability, company reputation, policies, etc.

Payments

Financial assistance, payment terms and methods, billing procedures, etc.

Remember that these are just general examples of some categories. You develop your own category list by putting yourself in your consumer's shoes and asking yourself, What would I need to know or want to know before I would buy this product? The number of category headings you have will naturally depend on the complexity of what you are selling and the variations of the product or service lines you offer.

This system assures that everything you want to say to any client will be at your fingertips. It serves as your own personal security system and will allow you to proceed with the confidence you need.

Once your information is categorized, it will be easier to learn and memorize. And that is your next step. The point here is that once you have the information compiled and learned, you can relax and concentrate on creatively delivering it to best sell your product as well as yourself.

. . . But Never Canned

One of the dangers, for novice salespeople, when delivering anything that has been memorized is that it can sound robotic and mechanical. One of the dangers, for even seasoned salespeople, in relating the same information over and over is that it can sound stale and dull. In both cases the presentation can come across as canned—rather than planned.

The following are four techniques that will enhance any basic presentation so it will come across as organized, planned, and informative, but definitely not canned. And yes, read on to see why women have an edge in executing these techniques:

1. *Tell stories*—There are many benefits to incorporating stories into your sales presentation.

- We tend to trust people who tell us stories. We were conditioned to do this from our youth. Think of the people who told us stories, such as our favorite relatives, parents, teachers, religious leaders, etc. All people we trusted. The connection between those who tell stories and those we trust seems to stay even as we mature. As discussed in Chapter Two, establishing trust is critical in sales.

- Stories have a moral, a message, a meaning, a point.

  The story: "Cinderella"
  The point of the message: Work hard, scrub floors, and someday you'll marry a prince.

  The story: "Snow White and the Seven Dwarfs"
  The point of the message: Always wash your fruit before you eat it.

  The story: "Goldilocks and the Three Bears"
  The point of the message: Watch whose bed you sleep in.

And since stories are usually about someone else (third party), they do not point a finger at the listener directly, but can still manage to get a message across. Getting your message across in a nonthreatening manner is essential in sales.

- Stories lubricate the memory like nothing else. It has been proven that when information is presented in story form, people remember facts and details that they normally would most likely forget. Since you'll want your customer to remember you and what you are selling, stories will definitely help in sales.

The bottom line is that stories make presentations more interesting. When inserted at opportune times in a presentation, they add an element of spontaneity. They can be used to shift a mood, ease the moment, provide credibility, and demonstrate your sensitivity and understanding of the prospect. For example:

"Mr. Bryce, your situation reminds me of something that happened to one of my neighbors recently. He found himself, like you, having to really decide between two courses of action. Let me tell you the story of what he did that helped him to decide . . ."

"I understand your concern, Ms. Robinson. A few months ago I was working with another client who felt exactly as you do. Let me tell you that story . . ."

"Mr. and Mrs. Davies, I know you feel that taking this step is difficult at your age. But remember, Winston Churchill did not become prime minister until he was way into his sixties, and Grandma Moses did not begin to paint until she was an octogenarian. As Mark Twain said, 'Age only matters if you are a hunk of meat or a piece of cheese.'"

Storytelling in sales requires an ability, interest, and willingness to make connections and seek out similarities, and we already know women are great at that. Additionally, women are comfortable with, and have a tendency to use, examples from personal experiences. The key is to have a story category in your presentation binder that includes a list of appropriate stories to demonstrate a point or get a particular message across.

2. *Personalize your presentation*—The world today has become amazingly impersonal—I haven't dealt face-to-face with a bank teller since 1989, I order lunch not from a waitress but from a machine covered with pictures of hamburgers, I drop my clothes off at a drive-through cleaners, and I can watch movies alone from my family room couch. It is easy to see that our highly technological world has done more to separate people than to bring people together. Every day we are confronted with new systems, devices, and gadgets that create a "removed," unconnected, impersonal feeling. Just last week I had an experience that demonstrated the extent of all the madness. I actually received a call from a computer. That's right, a computer dialed my number and a voice-activated machine asked me to take a survey. I was so appalled that I wanted to say, "hold on a minute . . . I'll let you talk to my blender."

People have a need—now, more than ever before—to feel that they are more than just a number, to feel a sense of identity, to feel that someone is relating to them on a nongeneric level, to feel like an individual. And if you are selling to these people, you had better understand this concept and consider those needs when developing your presentation.

Engaging in personalization during the course of your presentation considers those needs. Personalization as it relates to sales is all you do to make the customer feel you are talking to her and her alone. Personalization as it relates to sales is all you do to customize your presentation so as to connect your customer with the product on a personal level as well as with you.

Women (you read it in Chapter Two) naturally seek out ways to connect themselves with other people. And when it comes time to connect their product to another person, they have no trouble doing that either. Personalization comes easily to women.

By using their natural interest in making connections, along with some of the following personalization techniques, women can create a sales presentation that has impact and fills the needs of today's consumers.

- Insert short statements at the beginning or end of your planned remarks that make your message sound personalized. Statements like: "In your case . . ." "What might be particularly important to you . . ." "Since your company is based in several cities . . ." "Keeping in mind that you love to read historical novels . . ." "Considering your unique situation in that you just relocated . . ." etc.

- Refer to buyers by name and use the names of other associates or other relevant parties you are aware of. "Jennifer and Jason will love this room, won't they?" "Mrs. Carroll, your secretary, will find this a time-saving breeze," "I was glad that Herb Beamer gave me your name."

3. *Put yourself in the counseling position*—Since time is a shrinking commodity, especially in today's two-career and single-parent households, one thing most people are looking for is help. Help in terms of assistance, guidance, advice, or sharing a burden is a never-ending quest. We are constantly looking for help with our children, our homes, our yards, planning our future, coping with stress, and even in soothing our psyches. Help, however, no matter what form it comes in, seems to be another shrinking commodity. We are forced to pump our own gas, make our own salad when we dine out, catch our own criminals (TV's "America's Most Wanted"), and have even been instructed on how to be our own best friend (thanks to the book of the same name by Newman and Berkowitz). Yes, there is a problem today that we are all struggling with: Less time means we need more help, and good help is hard to find. Therefore, it is easy to understand why people are attracted to people who they feel can help them, and why consumers are attracted to salespeople who they feel can help them.

Women have traditionally been involved in helping roles—such as mothers, nurses, teachers, social workers, secretaries, housekeepers, flight attendants, etc. But it is not just our experience and training in "helping roles" that enable women in sales to project an appealing persona, it is that we convey the fact that we can help via our asking, listening, and relating skills . . . skills that make the customer feel we have an interest in her individual situation.

These skills are counseling skills and are used by the top counselors in order to diagnose, advise, and demonstrate their eagerness to understand the unique situation of the client. Since all consumers tend to feel that their situations are different or unique in some way, they, too, find someone who is willing to diagnose and advise very appealing. By projecting a counselor mode in sales, you let your customers know that you are a salesperson who is interested in tuning into their individual specific needs, wants, and situations. By using a counselor/adviser approach in selling, you will never be considered a mechanical salesperson with a generic presentation (a presentation that could be given to anyone).

In order to best place yourself in the counselor mode, three important steps must occur.

1. Ask questions with sincere interest in learning the answers. To do this you must demonstrate patience by not rushing the answer, indicating that you know what the answer will be in advance, or filling in the words before the customer is through. Additionally, you must use proper voice inflections that show interest. Making your voice rise at the end of a question shows not only interest but demonstrates enthusiasm. It also acts as a trigger to elicit a response. However, by dropping your voice at the end of a question, you come off as disinterested or prying.

2. During the asking segment of your presentation, you must actively listen to what is being said. You must limit your own talking and try to hear the ideas behind the words. Mentally connect what the consumer is saying to your own experiences. What you want to accomplish at this point is to **match** bits of information you are receiving with data and facts that you already possess about your product. To listen actively you must set aside your message and immerse yourself in your client's message (see Chapter Seven).

3. Be ready, willing, and able to confirm or clarify what you are hearing. True counselors in all walks of life earn the clients' trust by conveying a deep interest in understanding them. Phrases like "Do I understand you to mean. . . ?" "Are you telling me that. . . ?" "Am I correct in assuming. . . ?" all serve to demonstrate your interest in avoiding misunderstandings and in not misconstruing anything that might be important to them.

There is a big bonus in counselor selling. The salesperson who engages in counselor selling earns the right to lead the way and have her advice and suggestions accepted by the client.

Selling is a science because it involves organizational skills, fact finding, and adherence to a system that demands successfully completing one step before moving on to the next. But selling is also an art in that it involves flexibility, timing, uncovering relevance, storytelling, spontaneity, and creativity.

It takes a type of dramatic genius to sell. An effective salesperson must be capable of responding instantly and appropriately to the unexpected. An effective salesperson must be willing to create a new play with each "character" she encounters. An effective salesperson must appear to have an endless free-flowing conversational ability. An effective salesperson must be prepared to come up with the right answer, response, or means to handle a situation in a heartbeat.

THE BUYER'S TIME CONSTRAINTS

If you ask consumers to tell you their greatest fear in encountering a salesperson, you might be surprised at the answer. Most are not afraid that they'll wind up buying something that they don't want. Instead, I have found that most consumers' greatest fear is to be holed up with a salesperson for hours. They don't want to be with someone who will monopolize or waste their time.

Many consumer-expressed time concerns are genuine, but some are not. Though everyone seems interested in saving time today, as evidenced by fast food, quick relief, instant pudding, rapid transit, brief encounters, fleeting romances, and even microwave Minute Rice, some consumers use the "time" element as an excuse. They simply want to avoid dealing with a boring, overbearing, rambling salesperson who is operating on his own time agenda, not theirs.

Salespeople must be sensitive to the way of the world today and the genuine time constraints that people have. This may indeed require modifying or even rescheduling a presentation. But if the time constraint is an avoidance excuse on the part of the buyer, the astute salesperson must know how to test the consumer's interest barometer and "bait" the consumer enough to buy more time.

We already discussed (in Chapter One) women's ability to use time productively and to demonstrate flexibility and resourcefulness. Women also have a keen sensitivity to time and the time constraints of others. They are usually more willing to adapt to others' time agendas than men.

There are three steps that you must take with all consumers who demonstrate time constraints, be they genuine or just an excuse. Since women are sensitive in this regard, they should have little trouble deciding when to put these steps into motion:

Step 1:   Test the consumer's interest level with bait questions. Closed probes that are used for gaining control work well:

"Mr. and Mrs. Johnson, if I could show you a way to cut your food budget bill every month by 20 percent and have the brand names you want delivered to your door, would you be interested in hearing about it?"

"Ms. Smith, some of our biggest clients were once small companies. Would you like know how we helped them grow?"

"Mr. Phillips, if you send out more than five hundred pieces of mail per week, I can tell you about a time-saving system that's brand-new to the marketplace. Would you be interested in learning about how it works?"

"Ms. Jones, most people today are interested in keeping fit and healthy. If that is important to you, I have some information really worth listening to. OK?"

Step 2:   Determine the actual time you have with the customer by asking directly. If he is unable to meet with you at this time, but demonstrates interest—set up a second visit now.

"Can you give me fifteen minutes of your time?"

"It will take me just a half hour to show you the system. Do you have time today or should we set some time aside next Thursday?"

"How much time do you have before your next appointment?"

"Don't you think learning more about this is worth a few minutes of your time? We could meet tomorrow for lunch if today is too busy."

Once a time frame is established, be very careful to adhere to it. A consumer will distrust and resent you if you don't—but often give you more time if you do.

Step 3:   If they are willing to give you *some* time but not *all* the time you need, you must use a preplanned abbreviated presentation that will entice them enough to buy you more time—either now or at a later date. An abbreviated presentation does not mean a rushed presentation or one that will shortchange the consumer or your product.

An effective abbreviated presentation consists of:

- Three hard-hitting value statements about your product. The purpose of providing just three facts is to demonstrate your directness and your willingness to keep it brief, get to the point, and be businesslike. Also, three is a magic number in sales—there is a beat, a rhythm, a cadence to information delivered in groups of three. We use *three* hard-hitting facts because it has been proven that people remember things best in groups of three.

"We offer (1) fast service, (2) professional printing, and (3) reasonable costs."

"This home has (1) a wonderful location, (2) a huge backyard, and (3) that marvelous family room."

"This set of encyclopedias offers you (1) an automatic yearly update, (2) durable leather bindings, and (3) the most easy-to-use index system there is."

- A planned approach that encourages even the rushed prospects to do what they want to do the most . . . which is talk. The major misconception in planning an abbreviated presentation is in thinking that when time is scarce, you, as the salesperson, must cram as much information as possible into the time you have. In actuality it is just the reverse. The way anyone in sales can best buy more time is by letting the prospect do the talking. Although bringing to light three hard-hitting facts about your product may start the ball rolling, if you really want to pique the customer's interest, follow your three hard-hitting facts with open probes, questions like:

"How do you feel this product will help your company operate more efficiently?"

"Which of these three features would assist your staff the most?"

"Where are you thinking of setting up that system?"

- Having testimonials at hand from satisfied customers as well as warranty/guarantee information to refer to in your limited time. When buying confidence is down, as it is today, consumers want reassurances. That reassurance can come from company policy or from peer approval and reinforcement (others who have used the product or service you are selling). A good tip is to keep a variety of testimonials available so you can pull out those that best mirror the prospect you are now dealing with. This is one of the most effective means to buy more time today and to ward off a buyer's initial skepticism.

- Highlighting the comparative advantage of your product over the competition. In sales, we never say anything directly negative about the competition. It is just downright tacky, and only reflects poorly on you. Remember, "Every time you dig a little dirt, you loose a little ground." However, it is critical during the first four to six minutes of any presentation, and especially during an abbreviated one, to be able to bring to light why your product is *better* than all others. Statements like:

"Mr. Jones, I know your time is limited, but let me tell you what this VCR has that others don't."

"Ms. Johnson, I'd like to show you what our services include that makes us better than any other similar service out there."

"Ms. Green, I'd like to pinpoint what this insurance plan can provide you that no other coverage can."

These are comparative advantage statements that definitely get attention. They indicate that you have done your homework and have studied the competition. They make consumers feel that you have helped them in the buying process, by already doing some of the comparison shopping for them.

Yes, it is important for every salesperson to gather product information, to organize it, to learn it, and to prepare for spontaneity and flexibility in the delivery. This is what presentation development is all about. For a woman this is a cinch.

- 9 -
NOT JUST THE FACTS, MA'AM

□ □ □

REASON #9
Women Know the Benefit of Speaking in Terms of Benefits

Women, with their asking skills and motivating style, catch on to feature benefit selling in a snap.

Even Joe Friday, the famed cop on "Dragnet," knew that women have trouble sticking to the facts. Episode after episode we would hear Joe remind his female witnesses to deliver "just the facts, ma'am, just the facts." What may have been a problem with women for Joe is certainly not a problem with women in sales.

Actually it is the propensity that women have to elaborate and embellish on the facts that enables them to easily execute one of the essentials of good selling. That essential is the process of translating facts about the product's features into benefits to the customer. That process is based on the premise that people don't buy what it is, they buy what it will do for them. It is based on the premise that people don't buy the features of a product, they buy the benefits of the product. It is based on the premise that before your customer buys, she must be able to easily answer the question "What's in it for me?"

Understanding the benefits of what you are selling is critical to your sales momentum, your self-confidence, and thus, your ability to persuade. It is essential because it will provide you with a good feeling of knowing that you are selling something that has value.

110

As I just covered in Chapter Eight, it is your job as a sales-person to first gather the facts about your product. Then, however, you must be able to (1) determine which of those facts constitute positive features, (2) find as many benefits as you can that can be derived from those features, and (3) learn all the benefits so well that you can easily point out the feature benefits of your product that would be meaningful to your buyer. If you think consumers will effect this process of converting the feature into a benefit on their own during the course of your presentation, you are wrong. They are usually too busy thinking about other issues. If you think consumers will effect this process when they leave you and have the time to mull it over, you are wrong again. You see, once they are gone, if they think about your product at all, the likelihood is that they will be looking for reasons not to buy.

Yes, feature/benefit selling works especially well when the benefit is really targeted to the buyer. This concept hit home to me when I went out shopping for a new curling iron. I was looking for a good price, since a curling iron is just one of the many, many hair-grooming products I have to buy. (In fact, with all the hair spray, mousse, and gel I use, if someone lights a match next to my head—it could possibly explode.)

My first stop was a well-known beauty supply house. I asked the sales gal if she had any professional curling irons, and she pulled out two for me to choose from. My eyes immediately searched for the missing price tags. I questioned, "How much are these things?" She responded, "One is twenty-five dollars and the other one is thirty-five dollars." I asked, "What's the difference?" She replied, "Ten dollars." I left mumbling that I would have to think about it (I thought these things cost $14.95).

My second stop was a popular discount store. Approaching the hair-care department, I noticed the same two curling irons on a nearby shelf. Tracking down an elusive employee, I asked if those were the only two professional curling irons they had. She answered, "Yes, one is twenty-five and the other is thirty-five dollars." I followed with, "What's the difference?'' She answered, ''Well, the thirty-five-dollar one has a quick-heat-up filament, a Teflon wand, a no-tangle cord, a handy carrying case, and an automatic shutoff.'' Though I felt armed with a little more purchase information, I still had to think about it (I thought these things cost $14.95).

Third stop, a trendy new hair-care salon. Believe it or not, there were the same two curling irons displayed in the front case. A young woman with curls to kill for greeted me with, ''Oh I see you're looking at our curling irons.'' Getting right down to business, I asked, ''What are the prices?'' She echoed the twenty-five/thirty-five spiel, and I gave my line, ''What's the difference?''

CURLY SUE: ''The thirty-five-dollar curling iron has a quick-heat-up filament. You know what that means?''

ME: ''Sure, it means it heats up quickly.''

CURLY SUE: ''That's right, but because of that feature, you can sleep later every morning. You don't have to get up so darn early to plug it in. You like to sleep in, don't you?''

ME: ''You bet!''

CURLY SUE: ''It has a Teflon wand. You know what that means?''

ME: ''Yeah, it means the wand has Teflon on it.''

CURLY SUE: ''Yes, but what it really means is that your hair is protected from damage. Did you ever start curling your hair and you smell something burning?''

ME: ''Yeah.''

CURLY SUE: ''That's your hair burning, darlin'. Not good, makes it frizzy. You want nice smooth curls, don't you—like me?''

ME: ''Sure.''

CURLY SUE: ''Did you ever get your curling iron cord wrapped around your neck and you're thinking that your next curl might be your last curl?''

ME: "Every day."

CURLY SUE: "This curling iron also has a no-tangle cord. That will never happen. It's safe."

ME: "Oh."

CURLY SUE: "Do you travel?"

ME: "A lot."

CURLY SUE: "Did you ever think you might miss a plane while waiting for your curling iron to cool off so you could pack it?"

ME: "Just yesterday."

CURLY SUE: "I know travel can be tough, but this curling iron will make your life easier. You see, it comes with a handy traveling case that's lined with a heat-resistant material . . . so you can pack it up right away—still hot. Sounds good, huh?"

ME: "Sounds great!"

CURLY SUE: "One more thing. Did you ever leave the house in the morning and wonder, 'Did I turn that curling iron off?'"

ME: "Every day."

CURLY SUE: "You'll never have to worry. You see, this curling iron, the thirty-five-dollar one, has an automatic shutoff. If you don't pick it up in five minutes, it automatically turns itself off. Peace of mind, right?"

Of these three salespeople, who do you think I bought my curling iron from? The first sold price, the second sold features, but the third converted those features into benefits. She sold that curling iron *to me*. Did she do more than the other two salespeople? You bet! But just a little more. And that's all it takes!

Women, if you follow your instincts, you will find feature/benefit selling to be easy to perfect. Why? Think about the difference in the way men and women talk when they are trying to get someone to act on what they are saying. Men have a tendency to issue orders without explanation. A man will command, "Don't lean back in that chair." However, women, with their inclination to avoid confrontation and desire to create harmony and agreement, often soften their requests to influence action with an elaboration on the benefit of taking that action. For example, "Don't lean back in that chair, or you'll fall and split your head open." A father might command, "Brush your teeth." The mother will add on a benefit statement centered around a lovely smile and fresher breath.

I overheard a father in a convenience store warn his six-year-old son to stay put and don't wander. A moment later, as the child was wandering, the mother piped up with, "Stay put and don't wander so you'll be with us when we pick out the video." He heard the benefit and stayed right there.

Haven't you heard benefit statements like these from women all your life?:

"Eat those vegetables; they will make you strong and healthy."

"Don't run with a pencil in your hand; you might trip and poke your eye out."

"Wear that light blue dress; you'll really get attention."

"Don't go out with a wet head; you'll catch pneumonia and die."

Therefore, with product knowledge and some planning on your part, along with your feminine disposition to speak in terms of benefit statements, you can easily perfect feature/benefit selling.

There are three stages of developing the feature/benefit selling technique:

1. **Plan a feature/benefit list**
2. **Learn to target benefits**
3. **Understand how to best relate benefits to motivate the specific individual**

PLANNING A BENEFIT LIST

Take a look at the checklists that you compiled for your presentation development and jot down any and all benefits that one could possibly derive from buying a product or service with the features listed.

For example, as you look at the "company" checklist, you may notice that your company has operations in twenty major cities throughout the nation. Next to that feature, list the corresponding benefits, such as "Quicker delivery time," "Faster response time," "Product availability," and the like.

Finding the benefit of anything is quite easy. It simply involves examining a feature and asking yourself the question So what? or What's in it for the buyer? For example, for the thirty-five-dollar curling iron, the features and corresponding benefits might be listed as follows:

Feature	*Benefit*
Quick-heat-up filament	Saves time
Nontangle cord	Safer and easier to use
Teflon wand	Protects hair from damage
Auto turnoff	Allows a tighter, longer-lasting curl
	Peace of mind
	No fire hazard
Carrying case	Won't harm clothes in suitcase
	Packs easily
	Stows neatly
	Saves time—can pack away while still hot

Let's try finding benefits for the features of a different product . . . a car, for example:

Feature	*Benefit*
Tilt-wheel steering	Adjusts for comfort while driving
	Easy to get in and out of car
Antilock brakes	Quick stopping without skidding
	Peace of mind

Pinstriping	Aesthetically pleasing/Status
Included AC	Saves money
Fold-down rear seat	Provides comfort
	More carrying space
	More flexible space, etc.
Galvanized metal body	Sturdy
	Dent- and rust-resistant

LEARN TO TARGET BENEFITS

In order to do this most effectively, you need to have some insight into what your client is looking for and why. Everyone is an individual, and as such, has different needs and will benefit from your product in different ways. Therefore, it is important to remember that feature/benefit selling has the greatest impact when the benefit is nongeneric and personalized.

For example, if you are selling a home, you may be aware that your excellent location is one of your great selling features. Some benefits of that may include: good school system, easy access to transportation, convenience of nearby stores, low taxes, recreational facilities nearby, etc.

Now, really put your feminine questioning skills to use to uncover what specific benefit that location feature will have to your specific client. Suppose you determine that your client is looking at this location because of the school system. Your feature statement might sound like this: "As you folks know, this is a prime location that will afford you some wonderful advantages." Your benefit statement, however, might sound like this: "We have one of the best-rated school systems in the entire state, and in buying this home, you will be giving your children a wonderful opportunity. A top-notch school will not only have the curriculum to challenge them and keep them more stimulated, but will provide them with an edge that comes from having the best teachers possible."

Now, if the locational benefit to the next prospect comes from having access to transportation that will make it easier to get to work, your benefit statement will take a different turn. The feature statement can remain the same ("As you folks know, this is a prime location that will afford you some wonderful advantages"). However, the benefit statement will change. It may now become: "Being closer to transportation will shorten your commute to work, will afford you more time with your family, save you gas, and give you the opportunity to get a few hours more sleep each night."

A few years ago, when I was buying a car, I spent time with one salesman who was praising the power and quick pickup of the larger turbo engine that was a feature of this car. Unfortunately, I could have given a hoot about a car that went from zero to sixty in a fraction of a minute. I didn't buy the car from this guy, but I did finally wind up buying the same car from another salesperson. He made it seem almost like a different car by relating the same features to me in a manner that enabled me to connect with them. This salesman quickly realized I wasn't interested in a big engine for power. He therefore talked about the turbo engine feature advantage in another way—a way that I personally could relate to. He said that with the larger turbo engine (which evidently heated up rather quickly), I could turn on my heater on a cold winter day and be comfortably warm in a matter of minutes. He knew what I did give a hoot about.

UNDERSTAND HOW TO BEST RELATE BENEFITS TO MOTIVATE THE SPECIFIC INDIVIDUAL

Good selling requires a positive approach during all aspects of the presentation, but when translating features into benefits, there may be an exception. Although most people are motivated by benefits presented in a positive way, some people are more motivated by benefits presented in a negative way. The consumer who is motivated by the positive will respond to a statement such as "This lamp will provide perfect light for bedside reading." The consumer who is motivated by the negative will respond to a statement such as "This lamp will help you avoid eye strain while reading." The positive approach highlights the benefits to be gained from the feature, whereas the negative approach highlights the disadvantage you will avoid by having that feature.

Being an effective salesperson today demands that you make a quick and accurate assessment of how to phrase your benefit statement in the manner that will best motivate the buyer to take action.

To help you assess what motivates your client, you must ask pointed questions during your presentation and pay careful attention to what your client reveals through her answers. For example, let's say you ask the question "What is important to you in considering a new set of luggage?" If your prospect responds that she wants something easy to carry and expandable, she will probably also respond to positive benefit statements such as: "This luggage is lightweight and the rollers make it a breeze to use. Also, the side pockets easily open up to give you any last-minute extra room you might need." However, you would have to adjust your approach if your prospect responds to your question with a negative answer, focusing on what she *doesn't* want: "I want something that isn't going to wrinkle my clothes and doesn't take a weight lifter to move." In this instance you should appeal to her avoidance motivation and present your benefits with statements such as: "This luggage will not break your back, thanks to the roller system, and your clothes won't have to be re-pressed because these expandable pockets provide better protection from wrinkles."

There are two additional feature/benefit selling tips that sooner or later every good salesperson comes to realize:

Tip #1: *Don't fall into the trap of selling to others as you would like to be sold to.* How do you like to be sold to? Are you the kind of person who says, "I am looking for a dress that makes me look thin," or are you more likely to say, "I am looking for a dress that won't make me look heavy"? Are you more apt to request "a vacation spot that is easy to get to" or "a vacation spot that won't take me half the week to get there"?

Be aware that it is a natural inclination to present benefits to others in the manner that you yourself best relate to. Since presenting benefits in a manner that will most impact your particular client is important, practice relating benefits in both a positive and negative manner.

Tip #2:   *Try to make the benefits as immediate as possible.* Benefits that can be more immediately realized seem to make a further impact on people and influence more immediate action. The Downy fabric softener people learned this. They always sold an April-fresh smell, no static cling, and softness. However, sales supposedly really took off when Downy added the phrase "You'll see an immediate noticeable improvement in your clothes." Getting the immediate benefit appealed to people.

Texaco, too, learned the pluses of presenting to the consumer and immediate benefit of buying their product. Again, supposedly sales took off when they included in their slogan the fact that by using Texaco, you would immediately notice less engine knocks and pings.

So phrases like "The minute we install this computer modem, your life will be easier," "As soon as you start using this exercise machine, you will be on your way to a healthier body," and "You'll immediately feel less stressed when you start using the massage feature of this recliner" can be effective.

To reiterate, selling today involves helping the buyer see and appreciate the benefits of your product. So know your product features and learn their benefits. Use your feminine questioning skills to determine how to best present those benefits to your customer, and use your feminine disposition to speak in terms of benefit statements to motivate your customer to take buying action.

– 10 –
GIRL TALK

□ □ □

REASON #10
Women are the Great Communicators

Women love to communicate. They say we have the gift of gab. Since communication is what selling is all about, you can easily turn the gift of gab into a gift of gold.

S elling is communicating, and terrific selling is terrific communicating. And women, being the terrific communicators that we are, have yet another reason to become terrific salespeople.

The key in selling is to understand the old cliché. "It is not how many times you tell it—it is how many times you sell it." In other words, having communication skills that enable you to do more than simply converse, that help you to "*sell it,*" are essential in today's highly competitive business world. Yes, in sales, it is not just what you say, but the *way* you say it; it is the way you communicate that makes you memorable and unique, that stimulates and controls the interest of others, that demonstrates your credibility and belief in your product, and that enables you to get your message across.

Since most people can listen faster than they can speak, there is plenty of time, while you are speaking, for people to judge you and what you are saying, and to be affected by your communication style. There is also plenty of time while you are speaking for people to lose interest and focus their attention on something else. In fact, we can never assume that just because we are trying to communicate with someone, she has any interest at all in connecting with us.

There are innumerable stimuli vying for our attention every day, even in the most confined, controlled environments. Driving back from New York to D.C. last spring, I found myself stuck in a massive traffic jam inside the Lincoln Tunnel. Even here, in this stark, hazy cavern, I found that there were a multitude of things going on that commanded my attention. I noticed a tiny leak from the curved roof about twenty feet from me and started thinking what would happen if it got bigger. I wondered if the policeman patrolling on the side rails picked the shortest straw to get this post. Spotting two workers on the opposite lane fixing some tiles made me think of the cracked tile in my bathroom floor that I forgot to have fixed. In front of me was a van filled with kids flashing dirty hand signals to anyone who looked their way. God, did my kids ever do that? On the radio, which was fading in and out, was a famous talk-show host ranting and raving about some topic that I altogether seemed to miss. In back of me was a couple in a Mitsubishi arguing furiously; she seemed to be winning. I noticed a license plate on the car in the lane to my right that read "Live free or die;" I hoped it wasn't an omen. All of this, I absorbed in less than a minute. And these were just some of the external stimulations that attracted my attention in this seemingly limited environment.

I recount this incident to you to emphasize how difficult it is to keep our attention focused on any one thing. In sales, no matter how much someone may be interested in hearing what you have to say, or how effectively you are saying it, unless you are planning to set up shop in the Lincoln Tunnel, you are going to have to override many more distractions that will beckon your customer's attention.

Additionally, you must realize that people's natural inclination is to be more involved in themselves than in anything else. Also, people tend to fight off invasions into their personal realm of reflections and feelings. Especially in situations that can prove potentially uncomfortable, they try to remain detached and uninvolved. Cracking these initial natural defenses so that you can effectively communicate takes skill.

In this chapter I will cover some of the obvious as well as

the more subtle elements of effective communication mastered by successful salespeople to penetrate the *initial* walls of defense that all people build (that's before you hit the money wall). The eight elements can be implemented immediately by women to transform their already terrific communication skills into terrific sales skills.

1. ENHANCING YOUR VOICE

My grandmother, as perhaps did yours, reminded me repeatedly, "It's not what you say, it is how you say it." She, of course, was referring to choice of words, selection of phrases, etc. However, if you take this cliché literally, you have really hit upon an important yet commonly ignored aspect of communication. If speaking is your business and you want to be heard, how you sound when you are speaking is a very important self-assessment to make. The best way to really "hear" yourself is to listen to yourself on a tape recorder. Though you may have had this frightening opportunity already, you also probably dismissed what you heard by saying, "I don't really sound like that." Unfortunately, you *do* sound like that.

Yes, your voice as it is heard on a recorder is exactly the way you sound to others. When you hear yourself speak, you are hearing sound reverberations through bone; when others hear you speak, they hear sound reverberations through air. A recorder duplicates the way you sound to others. So there is work to be done to sound better—agreed? I am not suggesting that you should lose your unique identity and character, which are often conveyed through your voice. But to appeal to the broadest spectrum of people, you might find some voice training or adjustment worthwhile in terms of the following:

- **Pace:** The average person speaks at a rate of approximately 125 words a minute. I have been timed at 250 with word gusts up to 375. Yes, I still have a lot to learn about pacing; I am working on it constantly. Pacing, simply put, is the rate of speed that you speak. Remember, however, that the faster you speak, the higher the pitch, so all these voice elements are connected. Talking at a reasonable rate will help control your pitch.

Interestingly enough, there is a wide range that can be labeled as "reasonable" as far as pace is concerned. Matching your speaking pace to that of the listener would be ideal, (remember, we trust people who are most like ourselves). I have also discovered that the great speakers tend to talk faster rather than slower. Though I would never suggest that anything be done to project the image of the fast-talking salesperson, there is nothing more damaging to momentum and attention levels than a speaker whose sentences are punctuated with long ahs . . . and uhs.

Those of us who naturally speak too slow or too fast have probably heard about it from others by now. So if you have been told to "spit it out" or "slow it down," you have some work to do. If you want to be successful in sales—it would pay to do it.

- **Pitch and Inflection:** Pitch refers to your natural speaking tone. Your tone can make it easier or more difficult for others to listen to you. Usually lower-pitched voices are easier on the ears. Additionally, a variation in voice inflection (which is the rise and fall of your voice within your tonal range) is more interesting to listen to.

  Mastering inflections is a technique that many salespeople take courses in because proper inflection can demonstrate interest, caring, and involvement. Perhaps you have noticed that women's voices tend to rise at the end of sentences; it is an aspect of their natural inflection pattern. In sales you will find this not only useful in engaging in successful questioning, but it will help you immeasurably in handling objections, which I will discuss later on.

  Although it is well known that women have a higher speaking pitch than men, it is not as well known that they have a range of five tones to a man's three. With women's broader range of inflection and with some practice with a tape recorder on lowering your pitch, you have the potential to become both an interesting and easy-to-listen-to speaker.

- **Projection:** Projection relates not only to the volume of your voice—loudness and softness—but to the power of your voice that is achieved through breathing and control. A great actor like Sir Laurence Olivier could stand in the corner of the stage, literally whisper a line, and still capture attention and be heard effectively by his audience. Though the soft tones that women naturally have may seem more difficult to hear, in actuality, when fine-tuned, by learning to speak correctly through your diaphragm (not the contraceptive device but your muscles and tendons in your midriff), they can become more forceful and convincing than some of the louder tones.

- **Pause:** Pausing can be one of the most attention-getting and dramatic voice techniques or one of the most unnerving and distracting habits known. If engaged in at appropriate times, the pause gives the listener a moment to allow what was just said to sink in, enables you to set the mood for a point that deserves emphasis, and serves as a breather, an opportunity for you or your listener to digest information or mull over a remark. Keep in mind that a well-timed pause—a moment of silence—can be as captivating as the right words.

2. USING THE POWER OF DETAILS

My neighbor is nuts. She has a new boyfriend, and she insisted on telling me all the details about what happened when he came over last Saturday night (like I wasn't watching!).

Contrary to public opinion that details assure a yawn fest, details are actually what people want today. We as a society are very interested in the details of other people's lives, almost obsessively so. And getting on the bandwagon are not only publications like *People* magazine but the new TV shows that specialize in detailed exposés—all sorts and sordid.

Details, however, are not just appealing to the bored TV watcher, the vicarious liver, or the professionally unchallenged. In fact, details are appealing to everyone and have proven their worth in capturing interest, holding attention, and creating involvement. Just read even some of the more "newsy," staid, old-line, and reliable publications to see how details are used in so many of their stories to gain the attention of the American public. Yes, editors, publishers, producers, and advertising executives know the importance of details. And that message has value in all walks of sales.

There are two types of details that can enhance your sales power. There are people details and there are product details.

People details are details of a personal nature, information that reveals more about your customer so that you can better relate your product to him individually. Additionally, the sharing of details is necessary for intimacy and results in a stronger relationship bond. Studies have shown that women have a keen interest in sharing details of a personal nature. That interest often encourages others (both men and women) to divulge information that they would not necessarily reveal. So to really get to know your prospect and to develop a strong sales representative/customer bond, now is the time to bring this propensity into the workplace, into the field of sales.

Product details have proven to be what today's customers are looking for. In fact, the new selling style, as cited by many respected publications such as *Business Week,* clearly states that it is the salesperson's job today to be well acquainted with the details and subtleties of her product and well prepared to divulge that information as part of the sales process. Providing details in the sales arena is a way to not only establish credibility but to gain customer attention.

Just turn on your TV to your local home shopping channel for further proof. They need to have that product in front of your eyes long enough for you to convince yourself to get on the phone and buy it. They have got to hold your attention. And how do they do it? They do it with details. I mean, these people can talk about a simple black plastic ashtray for fifteen minutes. And they do. They measure it, give you the circumference as well as the diameter. They reveal the weight, height, and ash volume. They count aloud the number of recesses to hold the cigarettes, tell you where it was made, what it's made of, describe the luster of the enamel, and identify the exact shade of black by name. They provide details on how this black ashtray would fit in with any decor and even share with you the name of the designer, his native land, and his philosophy on function and form.

Women, as we have already discussed in Chapter Three, are accustomed to looking after, noticing, and dealing with details. This gives us an edge and one that we can use to perfect a presentation that will have credibility, hold attention, and provide today's consumers with one of the important things that they are looking for. Understand that I am not suggesting that your sales presentation consist of all the details you can possibly come up with; however, you must learn all the details and be able to expound on those that may be of particular interest to your customer at the time.

3. IMPACTING WITH VISUALS

Sometimes I feel that humankind really hasn't progressed as much as we think. Basically we still learn the same way that the caveman learned—by way of pictures. Granted, today's pictures are a lot more advanced than crude drawings on a dirt wall, but pictures, primarily those produced by television, still prove to be an incredibly influential educator.

Just to convince you of the extent of TV, the ultimate visual, as an educating power, I heard that only 6 percent of Americans know who the Chief Justice of the Supreme Court is, but 76 percent know who Judge Wapner is. (What really is scary is that most of those 76 percent think Judge Wapner **is** the Chief Justice of the Supreme Court. After hearing this, I was in a frenzy until I found out that William Rehnquist was the judge supremo.) Anyway . . . you get the picture?

Yes, the visual picture has proven to be an effective way to capture attention and get a message across. Getting people to see what you are talking about, not just hear what you are talking about, is essential. Since hearing is actually the least effective sense for memory, a salesperson who wants to communicate her message with impact and memorability must understand the power of the visual.

There are numerous studies that reveal the importance of the visual when it comes to educating. A study conducted by Northwestern University stated that when one adds graphics or pictures to a verbal or written message, it increases recall by 300 percent. Makes sense, doesn't it? After all, the nerve endings in the eye are much more numerous than those in the ear.

Additionally, the old saying, "Seeing is believing" has maintained its popularity for a reason. When we *see it*—we tend to *believe it*.

I spent several of my quality younger years reading *Photoplay* magazine. It is no longer in print, but it was the magazine of movie stars. At the back of *Photoplay* magazine they had several pages devoted to product sales. In practically every issue they had an ad for something called a "bust enhancer." It was a little plastic device that sold for about $9.95 and came in pink and blue (I always wondered why blue). It promised an enhanced bustline, and I, as well as a multitude of my friends, knew it had to work. They showed pictures to prove it!

As part of the ad there were two photos. The first was a woman *before* using the bust enhancer. She looked sad, had stringy hair, no friends, and of course, was flat-chested. The second picture was that very same woman *after* spending sixty days with the bust enhancer. She looked thrilled, her hair had volume, friends flocked around her, and she was voluptuous. I wanted to be voluptuous, too.

The pictures convinced not only me, but all the other girls in my crowd who bought this darn thing. I mean, pictures don't lie, do they? Unfortunately, that bust enhancer never worked on me. I can, however, out-arm-wrestle any guy . . . Maybe I was using it wrong.

The strength of the "seeing is believing" concept has been demonstrated over and over to me in my twenty-plus years as a sales trainer. Consistently, the highest producers turn to visuals whenever they can to heighten their message, attract attention, create memorability, and encourage belief in whatever it is they are selling.

Graphs, charts, pictures, articles that document a point, letters that serve as endorsements, slides, videos, illustrations, and the like must be included to educate, influence, convince, and persuade your customer to better understand and believe your message.

I know women don't mind collecting, organizing, and showing visuals on the home front. Who is the keeper of the family photo album, who carries the pictures in the wallet, who takes out the letter to pass around for the group, who arranges the slide show, etc., etc.? Now, of course, this doesn't make any statement about our ability to incorporate visuals into a presentation, but it does indicate we are comfortable sharing visual documentation with others.

4. ENGAGING IN REPETITION

Repetition has long been known to be an important key to learning. I still have vivid dreams of learning the multiplication tables by repeating them over and over and over again. Though I still am unsure on occasion as to what eight times seven is, I got all the others down pretty well. Well, the reputation of repetition is well founded. When I taught school in the sixties, though philosophically I strived for understanding of a concept, there was no doubt that repetition and drill entered into each and every one of my lesson plans. In fact, even the newer methods of education today that favor open classrooms and conceptual understanding above rote learning still find value in repetition as a critical learning tool.

Women frequently use repetition when communicating. "Clean up your room." "I said, clean up your room." "Did you hear me? I said, clean up your room!" When I talk about this aspect of our communication style in seminars around the country, no matter where I am, I note the bobbing heads of women in the audience who are vividly relating to my message and agreeing with my point.

Now, we could analyze our necessity to repeat until we are blue in the face, but the fact is that we women do it. By modifying this communication technique slightly, we can easily feel comfortable incorporating repetition into the sales message. I am not recommending that we say, "This product really fits your needs. I said, this product really fits your needs. Did you hear me? This product really fits those needs!" But I am suggesting that we can use our willingness to repeat the message, and by finding a few creative ways to rephrase, we really will reap the benefits of making a memorable point.

Over the years I have heard many facts about repetition. I have heard people say that one has to hear something six times for 62 percent retention, and I heard others who quoted seven and eight times is necessary for just 50 percent retention. The fact is that repetition is the key to retention, and if you want them to get the point and retain it . . . repeat it. I don't just preach this information, I *use* this information. Anyone who has ever attended any one of my seminars will readily vouch for my use of repetition. It works. It works. It works.

5. CONTROLLING THE ENVIRONMENT

There is no doubt about it, the environment can enhance the communication effort or kill it. If Steve and I have a fight, and he is intent on making up while I am hanging over the kitchen sink with a Brillo pad in my hand . . . fat chance. However, a communication miracle occurs if he decides to make up with me at a little Italian bistro with soft lighting, guitar music, and a bottle of Chianti. My mood changes, and it is not just the Chianti. I become a little more accepting, and his effort to make up is usually successful.

My point is simple but important: The environment, the atmosphere, contributes greatly to the impact of your words and the way your message is received. Now, in many cases you will be selling in the customer's environment and will have to put up with such decorator touches as marred knotty pine walls, folding metal chairs, and dusty artificial ferns. But if by any chance your customer comes to you and you are in control of the environment, enhance it. The benefit is far beyond pleasing the eye.

Women are sensitive to the environment and are usually interested in enhancing it. We are almost always the ones who select the pictures, arrange the flowers, and plan the furniture placement. We look hard and long for the right wallpaper, put up the curtains, and make the laborious effort to find a stain-resistant sofa fabric that matches. I maintain that though men may appreciate being in an appealing environment, the majority won't take the initiative to create it.

In your sales office, fresh flowers on your desk, a jar of hard candies, photos of your family, a feeling of warmth, and cleanliness do make a difference. Even wall colors can help or hinder your sales effort. The Wagner Institute for Color Research in Santa Barbara, California, issues a trends-in-color report, which will help you select colors for your office if you have any say in the matter.

The report shows that blue, though certainly the color most Americans prefer, discourages spending money. (My husband wanted every room in our house painted blue.) Cool green encourages spending money, warm green is institutional. Yellow, though it will attract attention, makes people restless and uneasy. Orange, though suitable for a fast-food restaurant, conveys a cheap or low-end image. Though black and red are power colors, sometimes they are overwhelming and should be used more for accents. The gray, white, beige, and natural tones, with suitable accent colors (especially cool green), are still trendy while creating an encouraging business environment. So if you have the power to paint it—paint it with the right color.

6. DRAWING ATTENTION TO YOUR MESSAGE

Setting up your prospect to pay attention to what you have to say can be done so easily. As documented by Pamela M.

Fishman of the University of California, women, in their natural speech pattern, more frequently than men begin sentences with the phrase "This is interesting." This phrase draws attention to what you are about to say and primes the listener to take notice. In the sales arena you can expand on phrases like this to include others, such as "This is really important," or "You'll be interested to know," which signal the importance of your upcoming remark.

7. AVOIDING JARGON

When I first moved to the Washington, D.C., area, I traveled the famed Washington Beltway practically every day. And practically every day I would see a sign that I thought must have been written in pig Latin or was some secret CIA code. It said HAZMAT CARRIERS USE RIGHT TWO LANES ONLY. Well, I didn't know what a hazmat carrier was, and certainly I was not going to show my stupidity by asking anyone what it was. So for years, whenever driving on that section of the Beltway, I stayed in the right two lanes, nervous that if I strayed, the police would pull me over, asking to see my HAZMATS. Maybe I was a hazmat carrier . . . I couldn't remember ever getting a hazmat inoculation. It took years before I luckily overheard that the sign referred to those vehicles carrying hazardous materials. (Now I speed in the left two lanes.)

I share this little incident to get across an obvious but so often overlooked communication element—simple, plain, precise speech works best. Yes, one of the quickest ways to get your customers to tune out what is being said is to talk over their heads or use words that they don't understand. Most salespeople are aware of this and try to use simple, straightforward language. This doesn't mean that you shouldn't strive for a better vocabulary, but it does mean that you'd better know when and how to use it. This also doesn't mean that you shouldn't familiarize yourself with industry terms. It does mean that you must exercise extreme caution when using jargon.

Many salespeople, as they become familiar with their product, develop a tendency to speak in a lingo or vernacular—very industry- or product-specific. They fail to take into account that the customer may not understand the terms, phrases, or jargon being used. Some seasoned salespeople have lost touch with this concept and miss out on sales with prospects who are too embarrassed or too overwhelmed to ask for explanations. Additionally, many rookies can fall into the jargon trap as well. In order to compensate for their lack of experience and in-depth product knowledge, rookies often try to use the few technical terms they have learned to show how much they know.

In both cases the consumer and eventually the salesperson loses out. Jargon does little to enhance credibility and much to distance you from your prospect.

Remember that selling involves a sharing of information, and it is up to you to do your part. Deborah Tannen in *You Just Don't Understand* cites that if women are focusing on connecting with others, they are more prone to feel the need to diminish the difference in expertise levels. Men, if focusing on negotiation, an important part of sales, are more interested in proving their expertise and more prone to playing one-upmanship. In light of this, in attempting to "connect" in a sales situation, a woman would be less likely to use jargon than a man. To reiterate, I am not suggesting you be ignorant of the jargon, just be sensitive to the potentially awkward position into which it can place your customer.

8. CONVEYING ENTHUSIASM, EMPATHY, AND CONVICTION

People frequently ask me if there is such a thing as a sales personality. In fact, this question has been tossed around among sales trainers for years. I have heard the gamut of responses, from those who profess that anyone with the proper training can become a success in sales, to those who say that there is definitely a sales personality type.

Though sales skills can be learned, I believe that there **is** a sales personality type. However, I feel that there really are only three personality traits that one must bring to the business of sales. These three traits cannot be taught, yet, to me, comprise the foundation of all good salesmanship. They are enthusiasm, empathy, and conviction.

No one, not even the best sales trainer in the world, can teach these characteristics. One can teach product knowledge, closing techniques, follow-up methods, and prospecting strategies—but one can't teach enthusiasm, empathy, and conviction. Yet all great salespeople have these three elements in their basic personality in one form or another.

Enthusiasm: Enthusiasm is not just something that is communicated to show your client that you like what you are doing; it is demonstrated to set an example for customers to follow. People learn by example, not by advice. However, I cannot tell you the number of times I have witnessed salespeople telling their clients that they should be happy or delighted with their purchase decision, while they themselves are displaying zero enthusiasm of their own. Customers need a guideline; they need to know what behavior on their part is appropriate.

I can recall countless times that my genuine enthusiasm at the thought of making a purchase was dampened by a blasé salesperson who, in neglecting to show enthusiasm, burst my buying bubble. Naturally, your level of enthusiasm and the ways you show it will depend on the product you are selling. But no matter what it is, from vacation packages to fertilizer, enthusiasm is needed.

Empathy: As *Psychology Today* reported, women are considered more empathetic than men—and what an advantage that can mean in selling. Yes, empathy, being able to put yourself in your customers' shoes, is a real advantage. It helps you see things from their perspectives and adjust your communiqué accordingly.

Conviction: Conviction in sales is a belief in what you are selling. You can try to fake it, but it won't work for long. The depth of your conviction will be one of the most powerful and persuasive selling tools you will ever own. Nothing you can tell people, no amount of logic or understanding, will help you sell your product better than your belief in it. Selling, in fact, is communicating your conviction to the customer. As Cavett Roberts, a motivational expert, says: "More people will be swayed by the depth of your conviction than by the height of your logic."

Enthusiasm, empathy, and conviction must be present whenever you communicate with a client. Though these cannot be taught, as I said, and must be already present inside you, knowing how important they are to the sales process should encourage you to allow them to flow naturally in all your communication efforts.

In sales you get paid to communicate. You must communicate everything from your product's strengths to your expertise to sell it. You must communicate in a style that is clear, precise, easy to understand, relatable, and dynamic. Women have strong communication skills to begin with, and can easily enhance their sales effectiveness with a developed consciousness of the effects of their voice, words, environment, and personal attitude.

THE WOMEN'S TOUCH

□ □ □

REASON #11
Women Know How to INvolve to OUTsell

Without involvement, there can be no sale. Women know how to create involvement in many different ways. Women's propensity to touch, their more emotional natures, their questioning skills, and more enable them to easily involve their prospects to buy what they are selling.

Though I was never what you might even remotely consider a scholar, especially in the field of science, I learned a scientific message as well as a sales lesson by reading a story about Galileo in Zig Ziglar's renowned best-seller, *Secrets of Closing the Sale*. It went something like this:

Galileo, remember him? He lived a long time ago in Italy, in the sixteenth century, and achieved fame for inventing the telescope. Well, this story makes him look a little less than brilliant.

First of all, you should know, Galileo was his first name, not his last. His last name was Galilei. Now, we could discuss that for a while, couldn't we? I mean, what mother would name a kid Galileo if her last name was Galilei? Tony, Mario, or Sal could have worked just fine. In any event, Galileo's family was of noble background. They lived in Florence, Italy.

Though they were not loaded, they must have been pretty well off. Old man Galilei had some clout in town, and Mrs. Galilei had some help in the house. Unfortunately, Galileo, though a good student with a wide variety of interests, had an inquisitive mind and was constantly bucking lessons taught in the local prep school.

Having the lira and the leverage, Mr. Galilei realized his son would benefit from a private tutor and hired the best—a disciple of Aristotle's, a gentleman who specialized in Aristotelian theory. Now, I am not talking about Aristotle Onassis here, I am talking about the real Aristotle, the famed philosopher, orator, mathematician, and physicist.

Supposedly, as the twisted tale has it, the tutor had a little trouble with Galileo. Galileo had a big mouth and disputed Aristotle's theories at every turn, especially the theory that had to do with (as we lay people call it) "falling bodies."

Now, I am sure that I don't have this exactly right (or even fundamentally right), but Aristotle had a theory of physics that professed that bodies of similar mass and density, but different weights, fall at different velocities. Seems logical, doesn't it? At least to me anyway. I mean, it seems that a big, fat tomato would surely fall either faster or slower than a small, light tomato . . . doesn't it?

Now, Galileo didn't buy this. He believed that bodies of the same mass and density, having different weights, still would fall at the same velocity. In other words, Galileo thought those tomatoes, when dropped from the same point, would hit the ground at the same time . . . no matter what they weighed. (I have since personally tested this falling tomato theory and am happy to report that Galileo was correct).

However, Galileo did not have much luck in convincing others of his theory. He tried, though. Supposedly he managed to gather the top professors from all the universities in the country at the Tower of Pisa on one sunny day for a demonstration. He climbed to the top of the tower (which was not leaning that much at the time) and spent about an hour dropping down objects that had the same mass and density, but that had different weights. No matter what he dropped—chunks of wood, hunks of metal, bits of paper, or pieces of pepperoni—it was clear that Aristotle was wrong and Galileo's revised theory was right.

The professors and wise men, who at first gathered reluctantly, ended up marveling at this discovery. They slapped their cheeks in amazement. They saw firsthand that Aristotle's theory, the theory they had taught in physics for all these years, was wrong . . . and that Galileo Galilei was right.

Unfortunately, those same professors, those same wise men, went back to their universities and, for the next fifteen years, even after seeing Galileo's dramatic demonstration, continued to teach, continued to preach, Aristotle's theory of falling bodies.

What went wrong here? Why was a smart guy like Galileo inept at moving people to action? Why didn't he have the power to persuade them to change? Why didn't he have the influence to get them to spread the word immediately? Or better yet, why didn't he have the ability to get them to go out and start using this new theory to start conquering new scientific worlds of their own?

You see, Galileo thought the facts and demonstration would speak for themselves. He thought the facts and demonstration would move people to action and persuade them to change their ways. After all, they saw it with their own eyes. They should have been convinced.

Boy, was he wrong! People need more than the facts to move them. People need more than a demonstration to persuade them. Here is where Galileo missed the gondola. He failed to recognize that though facts may get people to think, and though a demonstration can prove a point, it is involvement that gets them to act. And being aware of, or ignoring, this principle stymied Galileo's impact in the scientific world for many, many years.

Yes, had Galileo understood the principles that create involvement, had he taken the steps to include his audience in his demonstration, had he primed them to be receptive, had he understood what would motivate them, I am sure he would have *sold* his theory a lot earlier.

You see, it is downright easier to sell anything, be it an idea or a product, once your "customer" is *involved*. Yes, an *involved* customer is simply more likely to follow your recommended course of action . . . to buy what you are selling!

To be a good salesperson, you must know how to encourage involvement and understand that involvement can be created in three ways:

1. **Physically**
2. **Mentally**
3. **Emotionally**

Women, as you will see, have some special propensities that get others involved in all these three areas, quite naturally.

PHYSICAL INVOLVEMENT

By physical involvement we mean two things:

1. Physically involving your customer *directly with the product* through the sense of *touch*

2. Physically involving your customer with your *presentation of the product* through *activity*

Sense of Touch:
Touching = Involvement = WANT

Creating physical involvement *with your product* can be accomplished easily by tapping into the sense of *touch*. And don't the top marketers out there know this essential principle. *"Fifteen-day free home trials* . . . Send for it, try it, use it; if you don't like it, send it back and you still get to keep the bamboo vegetable steamer, Chinese wok, and steak knife set." Do you think they are getting many returns on a deal like this, folks? No way; the marketers understand the principle of involvement. They know that **if we touch it . . . we are much more likely to want to own it.**

Interestingly enough, most people are born touchers. Kids are always touching . . . always touching anything they can get their grubby little hands on. Perhaps it is their innate curiosity, but whatever the reason, touching does come naturally. Of course, intellectually we know that this is the way children learn. However, we, as parents, have still tried to browbeat this touching inclination out of them, because when kids start touching, it usually winds up costing us money. Either they break it, eat it, or drive us crazy till we buy it.

So parents have armed themselves with a litany of phrases to discourage this natural tendency. Phrases abound in our effort to get our kids to *stop touching*, phrases such as "Keep your hands in the basket," "I am warning you, don't touch a thing," "Must you handle everything?" "See that sign, HE WHO BREAKS IT, TAKES IT. If you touch it, you'll break it, and we're not taking it, so *don't* touch it."

Now, by the time those kids become adults, most have learned their lesson well and control themselves to the point that they just do not touch naturally anymore—unless they are greatly encouraged to do so.

Significantly, *women need less encouragement to touch than men.* Although, as children, both sexes touch, male touching, even playful touching, is aggressive in nature—wrestling, playing football, slapping their buddies on the back—while female touching is more harmonious—playing patty-cake, holding hands, and braiding each other's hair. Since the female form of touching can be more easily and acceptably transferred into adult society, perhaps this is one reason why women are more comfortable touching than men, whether it be an object or another person.

Since people learn from example and since it is easier for women to set an example of touching than men, we need to use this feminine propensity of ours to encourage our clients to touch our products as much as possible. *We must get them to touch . . . because that will get them involved!*

Therefore, no matter what you have to sell, getting your prospect to touch it will help her buy it. So encourage your prospect verbally and through example to:

turn the wheel

flip the switch

pull the lever

feel the nap

spin the dial

twist the knob

try it on

rub it in

slide it open

shake it out

slam it closed

spray it around

Yes, seize any opportunity to encourage your prospect to touch what you're selling! Remember: Touching creates involvement with your product.

Physical Activity: Physical Activity Buys You Time

Time is what a salesperson needs to sell a product. Time is what a salesperson needs to create enough value to justify costs. Since the salesperson needs time to sell, and customers today are very stingy with their time, once again, the salesperson must know how to *buy* time. A salesperson must know what it is that will keep the prospect interested and present.

Since it is a psychological principle that *disinterest is more likely to occur when there is a lack of physical involvement,* a good salesperson makes a concerted effort to keep her prospect physically active during the course of the sales presentation.

You see, if your prospect has an opportunity to just sit, vegetate, or be passive while you ramble on, the chance that you will lose her interest, attention, and focus increases immeasurably. When you have lost the interest, attention, and focus, you have lost the involvement and the sale.

Therefore, smart salespeople plan to give their customers a few little *activity tasks* to accomplish during the presentation.

Remember: These tasks assist in the involvement process. So to keep customers involved with your presentation, ask them to:

JOT IT DOWN
TALLY IT UP
SCAN THROUGH THE ARTICLE
FLIP THE PAGE
MOVE A BIT CLOSER
ADJOURN TO THE OTHER ROOM
WALK TO THE SITE
OPEN THE BROCHURE

Remember: Little activities can lead to big sales.

While men may be better at giving direct orders for action, women are better at making proposals for action. Males tend to request action in the form of a command: "Come over here," "Check this out," "Write this down." Women request action more in a proposal format: "Let's look this over," "Why don't you tally this up," "Can you open that brochure and follow along with me." The feminine format is less confrontational and, in a sales situation, will be easier for others to comply with. Yes, especially in a sales situation, in which a common customer fear is being under the control of the salesperson, this feminine "proposal for action approach" works better than the male "direct request for action approach" to defuse resistance, an insidious barrier to the sale.

MENTAL INVOLVEMENT

If the prospect isn't mentally ready to listen to you, the most effective sales presentation in the world will fall on deaf ears. Realize that although customers may be there physically and may appear to be paying attention, you must know if they are mentally ready to put themselves into the presentation. If they are not, it will be impossible for your presentation to impress, impact, or involve them. They must be willing and ready to:

LISTEN CAREFULLY TO YOU
CONSIDER WHAT THEY ARE HEARING
RESPOND CONSTRUCTIVELY AND HONESTLY
ENGAGE IN A GIVE AND TAKE
OFFER FEEDBACK
DEMONSTRATE PATIENCE
POSE THOUGHTFUL QUESTIONS

If they are not willing to do these things, you have a receptivity problem. If that is the case, it is your job to create a *heightened level of receptivity*, i.e., *mental involvement*.

Prospect receptivity levels vary during a presentation. This is a critical issue, often ignored by salespeople. Believe it or not, prospect mood swings can happen right before your very eyes. Even prospects who came in interested, or who set the appointment wanting to learn more, can in fact "fade out" right in the middle of your presentation through no obvious fault of yours. All of a sudden she remembers that she needs a new transmission for her car, he realizes his shoes are killing him, or she discovers her watch stopped three hours ago. Yes, all of a sudden self-involvement takes over—just like it took me over in the middle of the Lincoln Tunnel—except now it takes over right in the middle of your presentation.

Many salespeople are so wrapped up in their presentation that they fail to take notice of the client's "fade-out" of interest. Of course, before we can draw him back, we have to first realize that he's gone. Women, as you'll see in Chapter Thirteen, are more tuned in to social cues and nuances. Therefore, women have an advantage in gauging interest levels and will most likely find themselves observing the fade-out of interest rather quickly and in time to do something about it. This is a plus, because there is no use going on if the prospect is not with you.

But once the fade-out is acknowledged, you have to know what to do about it. Many salespeople just keep on talking, hoping that sooner or later they will hit on something that will make the prospect float back in and mentally rejoin them. This hit-and-miss approach does not work. However, if you stop your presentation until the mood swings back in your favor, you may be waiting until the swallows return to Capistrano, or the buzzards fly back to Hinckley, Ohio.

Understand that you, as a saleswoman, have the power to heighten receptivity or mental involvement. You have the power to keep them in the here and now!

There are two ways to increase receptivity or mental involvement:

1. Change your presentation approach from a telling format to an asking format.

2. Demonstrate your own level of receptivity.

The Asking Format

By asking certain questions, you cut through the prospect's preoccupation, and force him to think and respond. In essence, you get his attention back.

These questions are called *involvement questions*. Involvement questions are inquiries that are direct and specific. They beckon elaboration in that they are easy to respond to and require more than a yes or no answer. Additionally, these questions are similar to the ones that your prospect may ask himself after he buys your product.

Some examples of effective involvement questions are:

"Will this just be for your use, or will others be using it?"

"What are you doing now to solve this problem?"

"Which of these features is most important to you?"

"How do you feel that a product of this type would improve your operation?"

"What are you looking for in a product of this type that you don't have now?"

"When did you discover you would be needing something more efficient?"

"Where would be the best place to put this product in your office?"

Every salesperson has to develop a personal list of involvement questions that would best apply to the particular product being sold. From my observations, however, I have found that women are more inclined to ask *how, when, who, why, what,* and *where* questions. Women want details, and this questioning style fits right in with successful selling.

Remember: A highly receptive person is not necessarily a buyer, but he will give you a fair shake and try to understand and actively consider what you are selling.

Demonstrate Your Level of Receptivity

It doesn't end here. The truly effective salesperson carries this a step further and takes human nature into account. She realizes that a prospect is going to be more receptive to her if she seems receptive to the prospect.

Therefore, demonstrating your level of receptivity to your prospect is critical. That, too, can be accomplished easily by using *little power phrases that show your attentiveness and interest.* Phrases such as:

"Tell me more."

"Can you elaborate on that?"

"Explain what you mean to me."

"Expand on that point, please."

"Go on."

"I see."

"Continue."

These are little words and phrases that go a long way in displaying your level of receptivity. In women's favor, this is just another aspect of active listening. And since women are by nature active participatory listeners, we can use this to easily demonstrate our level of receptivity to our prospects.

As Dr. Aaron T. Beck says in his book, *Love Is Never Enough,* "Women also show a greater use of the pronouns 'you' and 'we,' which acknowledges the other speaker. This conversational style promotes a sense of unity." That feeling encourages prospects to be more comfortable, less adversarial, and more likely to elaborate and get involved once more.

EMOTIONAL INVOLVEMENT

Now, the process of emotionally involving your prospect with your product offering is a little more difficult to achieve. Though it is certainly started through physical involvement and enhanced through mental involvement, to actually achieve emotional involvement requires another step. It requires a higher degree of understanding and insight into uncovering the prospect's motivation and then the ability to build on that understanding through the use of motivational phrasing. To phrase what you have to say motivationally, use facts sparingly and emotion freely. Facts should be used to back up a point, but not necessarily relied on to motivate your prospect to action. Facts, as it has been said, have to be used in the same manner that a drunk uses a lamppost: for support, not for illumination. It therefore is up to the salesperson to "light-up" the facts enough so that action will follow.

Recognizing the feelings and motives of others isn't easy. It requires projecting oneself into another person's situation. Because women are better at understanding their own emotions, they are better able to understand and recognize the emotions and feelings of others. Additionally, since women have a heightened sensitivity to nonverbal cues, they are also better able to fill in the gaps between what is said and what people truly feel or mean.

So hey, let's admit to being the more emotional sex. And let's use it in sales to delve more, try to uncover more, use more emotional words in conversation, and to connect more emotionally with others. Tapping into and using emotion will help to better involve our prospects with whatever we are selling.

Ladies, sales is the business of persuasion. And persuasion hinges on the effective use of emotion. And emotion—that's an area we women really have locked up.

Smart people trying to sell anything to anyone are well aware of the importance of emotion. Smart people trying to sell anything to anyone know that seldom do people buy strictly on logic.

The message is clear and simple: Make sure you employ emotion in your presentations if you want to move your consumers to action. Yes, if you want to persuade them to buy what you are selling, use your woman's touch.

Uncover the Prospect's Specific Motivation

There are basically two driving forces that motivate a prospect to purchase a product: (1) the purchase will resolve a problem, and/or (2) the purchase will make the customer feel better. One or both of those reasons serve as basic purchase motivations for *all* prospects. However, the key in sales is to uncover the specific motivation: i.e., the specific problem to be resolved or the specific feeling to be achieved. Knowing the specific motivation and then playing to it will enable you to emotionally involve your prospect with your product. Uncovering the specific motivation requires three skills: asking, interpreting, and listening . . . and women excel at all three (see Chapters Six, Seven, and Thirteen).

To help you focus these asking, listening, and interpreting skills, understand that people buy things to (1) look better, (2) feel better, (3) perform better, (4) work better, (5) impress better, (6) secure better, and (7) live better. That is about it.

By asking questions beyond the fundamental qualifying probes, you can gain a sense of which of the preceding categories your prospect's specific motivations fall into.

Use Words That Play to the Motivation

Now, a prospect might have one or more of these motivations that they are hoping to fulfill with the purchase, but understand there are certain words that charge the emotions, depending on what the particular motivation might be.

For example, if your prospect is buying to **impress,** words like

accepted	top of the line
envy	upscale
prestigious	best
pride	luxury
esteem	respect
status	

will go a long way to emotionally reinforce involvement with your specific product.

If the motivation is **security,** words like

confident	protected
quality	safe
tested	guarantee
proven	reliable
assurance	reputable

will work well.

If the motivation is **performance,** words like

efficient	yield
productive	skillful
power	capacity
capable	dependable
competent	

will catch their attention.

Depending on the product you are selling and the prospect you are selling to, you will have to develop your own list of appropriate power words and use them to fortify the emotional side of selling. Be aware that there are some universal words that seem to tug positively on everyone's emotional side. They have been used in advertising and effective sales presentations for years.

> ## WORDS THAT CONNECT TO EMOTIONS:
>
> new, easy, free, improved, save, convenient, safe, happy, comfortable, proven, value, you, and love.

There are many ways to create emotional involvement through the use of words. So understand what motivates your buyer and then play to it with the right words. Words have power. They can conjure up images and good feelings, suggest solutions to problems, and create involvement.

Women have the distinct advantage of being able to use the physical, mental, and emotional to involve. Involving your prospect in what you are selling is the surest route to the sale. As Stephen R. Covey emphasized in his best-seller *The 7 Habits of Highly Effective People,* "Without involvement there is no commitment." Though he was not directly referring to product sales, his message still rings true. Getting the sale means getting a commitment . . . and getting a commitment requires involvement.

– 12 –
OBJECTION D'ARTE

□ □ □

REASON #12
Women Don't Object to Objections

Objections are a reality in sales. But they are also a sign of interest. Handling them is an art, but with women's interest in maintaining harmony and promoting a win-win situation, the mind-set is already in place for success.

From time to time, one of my dear friends, Laura, who is out there in the singles world, tells me about her escapades. Actually, we spend a lot of time talking about the bar scene and how much she hates it. In fact, during our last conversation on this topic, she vowed that she was never ever going to a singles bar again.

I phoned her just recently and got an earful. It seems that one of her other female friends attempted to coerce her into giving a local watering hole one more Friday night try. Laura stuck to her guns for a solid two minutes and then, realizing she had nothing better to do that night, agreed to meeting for one margarita and then home.

Laura walked into the bar looking for her friend. Scanning the crowd and checking her watch, she realized she was early. She elbowed her way up to the bar and ordered that frozen margarita. While waiting for the bartender to blend the concoction, Laura felt someone staring at her. She looked up and directly across the bar was *the man of her dreams.*

Laura described him as sensational. She played it cool. Smiled coquettishly, but minimized the eye contact, so as not to look desperate. Once the drink was served, she squeezed away from the bar and made her way through the crowd to find a table and wait like a lady for her girlfriend.

The man of Laura's dreams, however, followed her. He, too, carried a frozen margarita, and though this was a premature assessment, Laura thought this might have been a match made in heaven, since they obviously had a great deal in common.

Still playing it coy, Laura momentarily let her mind start thinking good thoughts. Maybe, just maybe, this guy would be different. Not the typical bar fly.

Taking a seat at a table for two, Laura barely got situated when *he* appeared, standing over her with a Tom Cruise smile. "Hi, I couldn't help but notice you the moment you walked in. My name is Art."

Laura thought, "What the heck, I'll go along with it." She said, "Hi, I noticed you noticing me. My name is Laura."

Art took an uninvited seat and they bantered back and forth quite easily for seven to eight minutes. Laura admitted that her judgment of time was probably impaired by the luster of the night and the tequila in the drink, but she assured me the conversation never reached the ten-minute mark.

Then, out of the clear blue, the man of Laura's dreams looked at her and queried, "Laura, will it be your place or mine tonight?"

How suddenly can a dream vanish? How quickly can the luster tarnish? How stupid to give this "scene" one more try. How many calories were in this dumb drink?

"Who the hell do you think you are?" erupted Laura. "Just who the hell do you think you are? I met you seven minutes ago and you have the audacity to ask me that question? What kind of person do you think I am?"

Art sheepishly stood up, but he did not exit. He looked at Laura and said, "I'm sorry, Laura. I misunderstood. I can see now what kind of person you are. You sure are a different type of woman than the type I usually meet."

Laura responded, "I'm glad you're getting the picture; now, take off!"

Not taking off, Art continued, "A woman like you . . . what are you doing here?"

"I'm just waiting for my friend, so please leave," spurted Laura (but this time the eruption had less force than the first.)

"You're different, Laura aren't you," asked the still present Art.

"You bet I am," beamed Laura. "Yes, you're different; I know that now and respect you for that. Can we just talk until your friend comes? I really enjoyed our conversation before."

It really frosts me, but . . . where do you think Laura spent the night?

Now, there are many more details to this story, but since I would still like to keep Laura as a friend, I won't share them with you here in print.

What happened here? Though this incident may not on the surface directly correlate to the type of "sales" we are talking about, there is a message here that applies to anyone trying to sell anything. The message is that handling resistance and handling objections are almost always part of the sales process, no matter what you are selling. And creating harmony is an important prelude to handling those objections.

THE CONCEPT OF HARMONY TO DEFUSE OBJECTIONS

An objection, as it applies to sales, basically refers to a feeling or expression of dislike or opposition by the consumer in regard to the product you are selling. Art was trying to make a "sale" (himself). Laura had an objection. Art used harmony as a first step in handling Laura's objections.

Now, you may be thinking (or screaming), "Art is the master of the snow job." And you would be right. Art was not genuine, and his approach, though it worked, was manipulative and insincere. (Note Art's magic only worked on Laura for one night. He'd never make another sale to her!) Women, however, as you will see, are generally genuinely interested in creating harmony. Once again we have a powerful tool to use in the world of sales, so let's explore a bit further how this works.

A feeling of harmony can be created in many—and sometimes the most unlikely—ways. Study the panhandler. Panhandlers reveal their experience level very quickly. The new guys on the street try to stop you, block your path, while they beg you for the buck. But the pros go about it a little differently. They never try to stop you or block you. They see you coming and they fall into step with you. They walk right along with you and move *with you*, not against you, sometimes for blocks. And are they successful? You bet they are. They do the same thing as Art did on a little different level (a higher one). They create an avenue for harmony, they get in step. Art's harmony came verbally, through agreement. Professional panhandlers create harmony physically by getting in step with their mark.

In sales, when objections are raised, or you meet resistance of any kind, fighting back by trying to block your customer's reasoning path or by hoping to eventually wear your customer down to see your point of view will not work. Instead, you must begin by finding areas of agreement, paths of harmony, that will serve as a prelude to whatever method you use to handle the objection eventually.

Women are extremely willing to go out of their way to create harmony and to keep in step. Women favor a win-win approach to conflict resolution, whereas men with their more competitive natures frequently engage in a win-lose approach.

When it comes to harmony, women are more inclined to be the peacemakers and to promote cooperation rather than competition. Men by instinct are more dominant and competitive in relationships; these traits just can't help but come out in a sales situation in which conflict in the form of objections is a part of the buying process.

Yes, a customer objection creates an opportunity for conflict and confrontation or, on the other hand, reconciliation and arbitration. Men are more inclined to confront, and women are more inclined to reconcile. Because of socialization and biology, men are more inclined to want to win by dominating, and women are more interested in winning by cooperating. The softer, less confrontational approach is exactly what is needed in sales to defuse your customer's objections.

HOW TO SET THE STAGE FOR HANDLING OBJECTIONS

- *Get in step* with your customers by using little phrases that demonstrate you heard what they said, cared what they said, and don't think what they said was stupid:

  "I appreciate your comments."
  "I understand your point."
  "I see how you feel."
  "I know what you mean."

These are important phrases that show you respect the consumer's right to an opinion.

- *Clarify* by nonconfrontational questioning to make sure you understand the objection:

  "So I understand how you feel; *you are telling me that . . .* "
  "I see how you feel; *in other words, you are saying that . . .* "
  (Here you restate the objection in a questioning, nonconfrontational tone. By doing so you turn it into a probe that demands more specific elaboration.)

Voice inflection here is very important. Throwing back what was heard in a questioning tone makes the customer have to defend her position. "I understand what you are saying; in other words, you feel you need a machine with more power?"

- *Redirect the objection* by building a bridge that will enable you to move on: Proper bridge words are important to continue to assure harmony with your customer and to position yourself for handling the objection. Bridge words such as the following work well:

  "However" (as in "However, have you considered . . . ")

"*Yet*" (as in "Yet there is another aspect of this that you might not have thought about . . . ")

Avoid using the word "*but*" as a bridge word as it negates any positive and sets up consumer defenses ("You have a great personality, but . . . "). With the word "but," the compliment is negated and harmony is lost.
Example:

SALESPERSON: "I understand what you are saying; in other words, you feel you need a machine with more power?"

CUSTOMER: "Yes, I am afraid this will not be able to handle the workload in a few years."

SALESPERSON: "I see; *however, based on your current needs and budget, consider . . .*"

WHAT AN OBJECTION REALLY IS

Many salespeople shudder at the thought of objections, but usually it is because they don't understand what objections really mean or their significance in the sales process. On a psychological level, objections have been proven to be a sign of interest from the consumer. They are a natural step in decision making. The novice salesperson fears them, the expert welcomes them. They indicate involvement and beckon your interest and sales expertise in helping the consumer find a reason to buy.

For example, if I am out shopping for a dress, I move the items along the rack with incredible speed. I know what I am looking for. The saleswoman stands six feet away. She watches me whiz through her stock. All of a sudden I remove a dress from the rack, hold it up, and comment, "What a funny color . . . I can't imagine who would want a dress in this shade."

The average run-of-the-mill salesperson thinks, "She ain't buying that one." The smart, experienced sales professional thinks, "Bingo . . . that's the one she's going to buy, but she needs to work out the objection first, and I'm going to help her do it." She says, "Oh, yes, that color is a bit unique, yet an interesting designer choice. It really can go with so many other colors. Don't you agree?"

In other words, objections are not stumbling blocks to the sale. Instead they are usually a signal from consumers that they need your feedback, they require reassurance, they want justification, they crave a sounding board, they want more information, or they desire elaboration.

TECHNIQUES TO WORK THROUGH OBJECTIONS

During my sales training sessions I teach several ways to work through objections. In fact, I have come up with an acronym that covers several of the most effective ways. That acronym is the word D-I-R-E-C-T.

D—Stands for *Diverting*. "Ms. Jones, though you are not sure of the feeder, you do like that collating feature, right?" In actuality what you are doing here is diverting the customer's attention from something she perceives as a negative to something she has already accepted as a positive.

I—Stands for *Ignoring*. "I understand what you are saying about the color of the machine. How many copies did you say you put out on average each month?" The philosophy behind this technique is that often the consumer will forget about the objection, work it out in her own mind, and never be bothered by it again.

R—Stands for *Realigning* the cost-to-value ratio. "I appreciate that this may be more than you intended to spend. Tell me, *how much more* is this than you wanted to spend?" After consumer's answer: "Ms. Jones, that boils down to ten dollars a day for a machine with better collating power, faster processing, and clearer reproductions. Clearly you can see that for a few extra dollars you will be getting so much more." This technique is intended to build value to justify cost. It puts emphasis on the value side of the cost-to-value ratio.

E—Stands for *Establishing Evidence*. "Mr. Johnson, I understand your concern; that's why I'd like you to take a look at these letters that I have received from customers just like you who were concerned about clarity." There are several ways to establish evidence to support your words as a salesperson. Letters from satisfied customers with similar concerns, documentation in the form of articles and other proof sources, as well as warranties and guarantees, all serve to allay concerns that surface as objections.

C—Stands for the *Compromise*. "I know you are looking for the top of the line, Mr. Jones; however, this mid-range model offers so much, and the monthly payments fit right in with your budget."

Sometimes the objection must be handled with an acceptance solution presented in the form of a compromise. That involves simply taking the time to detail to the consumer how, though the solution is not perfect, the positives outweigh the negatives.

The compromise, one of the top techniques in working through objections used by salespeople, may be presented in written form. For years, salespeople have been using what is called the *Ben Franklin checklist*. (Supposedly Ben used this system to make decisions when he wasn't flying his kite).

In any event, it involves working with your customer to record on paper both the positive and the negative aspects of the purchase. As the salesperson, you should be well armed to assist your customer with the positives, to be able to fill in on the plus side. Let the customer, however, work on the minus side without your help. If you have done your homework, the benefits of your product will far outweigh the negatives and the customer will see that the compromise is worth it.

T—Stands for the *Turn-around.* You are in an ideal position if you can turn the consumer's negative concerns around to highlight a positive benefit of your product. For example: (the client) "No basement . . . This home has no basement?" (the salesperson) "No, you are right Ms. Fallman, this home doesn't have a basement. However, keep in mind that if storage is what you are seeking, the attic and shed will provide a great deal of space. A basement, on the other hand, can really serve to be a collecting place for junk. But additionally, with Timmy's allergies, you will appreciate not having the damp breeding ground that doctors warn about." The turnaround technique is the most powerful of all. It does more than provide a positive to counter a negative, it actually turns the negative into a positive.

THE MOST COMMON OBJECTION HEARD—PRICE

In most cases the objection you hear will revolve around price. It is critical to learn how to handle price objections and to maintain a positive, nondefensive role in the process. Many amateur salespeople try to apologize for price, when in actuality the true professional knows how to realign the cost-to-value ratio and position themselves to brag about it.

I cannot help but refer to one of my trips to Hong Kong. Now, being the shopper's haven that it is, I am certain that the salespeople are well armed and equipped to handle price objections. (Hong Kong is not the bargain mecca it once was.) However, I really was bowled over by the salesperson I encountered at Sebu, one of the most popular stores in Hong Kong. Here's what happened.

I approached the silk scarf counter with trepidation, knowing that these items would probably cost more than I wanted to spend. The saleswoman, quite an expert, showed me a wonderful scarf that cost a fortune. I told her I loved it but indicated that it was about forty-five dollars more than a similar scarf I had seen at the Stanley Market (another shopping area).

Her tactic was interesting. Did she try to tell me I was wrong? No. Did she try to tell me I was crazy? No. Did she lower the price? No. Did she offer to sweeten the deal with a matching doily? No. She looked at me and with all sincerity said, "Oh, I am certain you saw a similar scarf at the marketplace for forty-five dollars cheaper; however, *this* scarf, I assure you, is forty-five dollars better . . . and let me tell you why . . ."

From that point on she went on to expound on the quality of the dye, the intricacy of the design, and the fact that it was hand-rolled. She built value . . . value in the scarf. And, building value is one of the most powerful techniques anyone can use against the price objection. Along this same line, it is critical in today's world to be able to readily explain to today's consumers the difference between price and cost. My godson wanted a Mongoose for Christmas—I thought it was a pet, but found out it was a bike. Out shopping, I realized that I did not want to spend what they were charging for a Mongoose. Unfortunately, the cheaper one that I finally bought broke the third time he rode it and cost a great deal more in the long run due to the repairs. The consumer must be made to understand that price is a onetime issue, but cost is something that you live with every day that you own the product.

Most buyers can understand the difference between cost and value, as well as the difference between price and cost, once an expert and prepared salesperson highlights the differences.

This brings up the topic of being prepared, which is probably one of the key elements of handling objections effectively. It is amazing how many salespeople have to reinvent the wheel because they never take the time to research and plan an effective response to objections that they hear over and over again.

TIPS TO MAKE OBJECTION HANDLING EASIER

Tip #1:   List any potential objections that you recognize while learning about your product and think of the technique that would work best in helping you to overcome them.

Tip #2: Keep a log of every objection that you hear from a customer and make sure that when you hear it the second time, you are prepared to handle it.

Tip #3: Though it is wise to become familiar with potential objections that may surface about your product, avoid the urge to anticipate them, as that telegraphing can bring to light something that otherwise would have been passed over. My mother-in-law is a big anticipator. She rings my bell and says, "Darling, I brought you a present. If you don't like it, you can return it. In fact, I knew you wouldn't like it, so I returned it already."

Tip #4: The interesting thing about objections is that sometimes salespeople think that they have to solve them on the spot. It is not always true, and often by just "holding hands," or expressing a willingness to work on it, you can set the stage for the eventual sale. Men have a hard time with this as they tend to see things as black and white. It is either "go" or "no go." Women are not as willing to throw the baby out with the bathwater. They don't look upon things as strictly black and white and are willing to hold down the fort and not give up without engaging in some additional work.

Tip #5: Occasionally an objection is raised that you simply will not be able to handle at all. What you are hearing may not be an objection, but actually may be a condition that makes it impossible for the prospect to buy what you are selling at this time. It is your job to decipher a condition from an objection and realize that a condition usually is a complete block to the final sale, and one that you must again be prepared for . . . prepared to walk away from.

P.S. Ladies, Art is still out there . . . He is something to walk away from, too.

– 13 –
THE MESSAGE BEYOND
THE WORDS

□ □ □

REASON #13
Women Have Intuition and Use It

*If the saying, "buyers are liars" has truth, women
are lie detectors! In the field of sales, women can
use their ability to read signals to develop a more
complete picture of what is occurring in the mind
of the buyer.*

In the old school of selling there was a cliché, "Buyers
are Liars." I was always uncomfortable with that phrase
because it labeled buyers as devious, underhanded, and
deceitful. Now, having a black belt in shopping myself, I
tended to take this negative stereotype of a buyer quite personally. Though I never took it so personally as to actually
stop shopping, I did take it seriously enough to stop to ponder what prompted this sales paranoia. I concluded that *buyers often appear to be liars because:*

- When they say no, they don't always mean no.
- When they say they are "just looking," they often buy.
- When you ask them what they want, they give a vague
  answer.
- When you show them *just* what they wanted, they don't
  seem to want it anymore.
- When they say they want one thing, they often wind up
  buying another.

Expert salespeople soon learn that:

- Customers often say "no" instead of "I don't know," or in place of "You haven't given me any new information to help me change my mind from a no to a yes."

- The "just looking" phrase is a reflexive consumer response to the "May I help you" phrase, which is a reflexive sales opener.

- Vague answers are often the result of confusion, inability to *express* what one really wants, or uncertainty as to *what it is* that one really wants.

- Feigning disinterest is a common consumer defense mechanism to slow down the buying action and to avoid being marked as an easy sell.

- Specifications and motivations are two different things. And though some consumers may easily be able to spout out their specifications, they very often buy based on their hidden motivations.

> *Specifications*: "I want a mink coat on sale, with female pelts, a rolled collar, wide cuffs, and a midcalf length."
>
> *Hidden motivation*: "I want a glamorous look."
>
> *Purchase decision*: The floor-length ermine coat sans collar and cuffs—full price.

So as we learn more and more about the psyche of today's buyers, we realize that *buyers may appear to be lying when in actuality they are:*

- Confused about what they want
- Unable to express what they want
- Sure that you must already know what they want
- Afraid to show how much they really want it
- Determined not to buy something that they don't want

In addition to that, most prospects:

- Rarely volunteer information
- Tend to talk in generalities
- Perceive things differently than you do

So what are we supposed to be in sales—*mind readers?* You bet, and luckily, that's exactly what women are. Yes, women have the ability, the sensitivity, and the interest to hear beyond the words, see beyond the pictures, fill in the blanks, detect the cues, piece together the clues, and know the unknowable. Women have intuition!

"Women's intuition," which was the label given for women's quick insight and ability to accurately judge a situation or person based on limited information, has been much maligned. This beneficial feminine trait was until quite recently ignored in the business world, and the emphasis was placed entirely on rational thinking, to the extent that businesspeople had a hard time admitting that they ever used intuition at all.

Many of the most pragmatic and rational thinkers in the business world today, be they men or women, may deny that they use intuition as part of their decision-making and problem-solving repertoire. But these same people seem to have no problem at all admitting and even touting their keen "business sense." Well, you can call it "business sense" or you can call it "intuition." No matter what, it is one and the same.

WHAT IS INTUITION REALLY ALL ABOUT?

Intuition is the result of one's ability to transfer the information, feelings, thoughts, and impressions gleaned from one experience or situation to another experience or situation without the use of rational thought. Intuition relies heavily on one's willingness and inclination to trust one's own "feelings," to go with one's "guts," to follow a "hunch."

HOW DOES IT WORK?

Intuition starts with a genuine interest in or sensitivity to a specific subject matter, experience, or situation. For example, my younger son Mitch, has an interest in cars. Out of this interest grew an understanding of how a car motor works. One day when my dishwasher broke, my son and I were both shocked to discover that he knew how to fix it. The impression, feelings, information, that he had gleaned from working on car motors assisted him with the task of rooting out the problem with the dishwasher motor. In other words, he had the ability to transfer his knowledge of motors from one situation to another.

Now, some people may call this simply a transfer of learning, which it is. Some people might call this having a mechanical sense, which it also is. But no matter what you may call it, my son had a "hunch" as to how to fix that motor without studying the manual. And that hunch was based on what he knew about motors already. And what he knew about motors already started with his interest in that subject.

So you see, intuition is really a hunch based on past information, feelings, impressions, that all starts with interest in a subject or sensitivity to a subject.

Both men and women have hunches. But women basically are:

- More interested in human interaction than men
- More sensitive to human relationships than men
- More attuned to the workings of people than men
- More in touch with their own emotions and feelings than men

Having that interest and that sensitivity, and being more at-tuned and in touch, enables women to:

- Recognize nonverbal signals more quickly than men
- Cultivate "hunches" about people more easily than men
- Intuit feelings of people more accurately than men
- Act on those hunches and intuitions more comfortably than men

Taking the first step of recognizing nonverbal signals is essential in developing people intuition. My experience has proven that most men don't have an interest or a clue when it comes to picking up on nonverbal signals. Whereas women have a full-blown antenna, men seem only to have a coat hanger with a little piece of aluminum foil wrapped around it. My feelings about this have been corroborated by many women all over the world who tell me stories of "male missed signals" that would make your hair stand on end.

I have one friend in particular who seems to have a terrible time ending relationships. She is basically nonconfronta-tional and tries to be delicate, but when her hints get ignored, she eventually finds a desperate need to be more and more blatant with her "let's call it quits" signals. In fact, she swears that in order to break up with her current boyfriend, a com-mander who should remain nameless, she is going to have to learn to spell out "Pack your duffel bag and get out of here" in navy flags. Now, this may sound extreme, but you don't know Commander Vernon Duane Toderro like I do. Additionally, I am sure that when the flags have been waved and he finally gets the message, his response will be, "What, are you kidding? I thought everything in our relationship was going great. I mean, is there a problem?"

Women, on the other hand, are quite sophisticated in de-tecting nuances, divining motives, and interpreting the un-derlying messages of others through the use of their intuition. Women have the ability, sensitivity, and interest to decode what people are feeling, to learn what they're about, not only based on what they say but from reading nonverbal signals, i.e., body language and emotional undertones. Women's ability to decipher nonverbal cues was confirmed in a study conducted by a team of five researchers from Harvard, John Hopkins, and the University of California in a 1979 study titled "Sensitivity to Nonverbal Communication: The Pons Test."

Picking up on cues, picking up on clues, reading the signals, putting two and two together; women are masters at it. Steve and I go to a cocktail party and meet a couple for the first time, by the end of the evening, without asking, I know what type of underwear he wears and their china pattern.

Now, this gift isn't mine alone. Women naturally rely on facial expressions (for example, the grimace from extratight Jockeys), posture, and eye contact, as well as voice inflections to read between the lines. Women also tend to pay closer attention to how people interact as well as to what they have to say. Yes, women have the inclination and the ability to read *beyond the words*. And this is exactly what we need in sales.

Sales is a people business. Getting to know your prospects, being able to read their unspoken messages and to interpret their often cryptic signals, is what it's all about!

In the field of sales, women can use their ability to read signals to develop a more complete picture of what is occurring in the mind of the buyer. How is she relating to the product or service? What does she really think of the price? Will the product or service fill her needs? Is she convinced of the value? How close is she to making a decision?

Yes, zeroing in on the emotional undertones and nonverbal cues and transferring past experiences to current situations can help uncover feelings and information you can use to bring you closer to the point of sale. Additionally, there are some definite signals that experienced salespeople have come to recognize that will help you better assess the buyer's interest level and detect how close he is to making a buying decision. Add these to your already astute people-reading skills, and you will develop a true selling advantage!

Buyer Signals

When consumers are close to making a decision, they display similar signs and body language cues that demonstrate their interest level, buying comfort zone, and readiness. These, we'll call *buyer signals*. Some indicate a positiveness, a willingness to proceed with the sale. Others indicate a hesitancy and concern about making a purchase decision for one reason or another.

So let's now look at some common buyer signals, learn what they mean and how to capitalize on them. Remember, though these signals may appear at any point in your presentation, they have special meaning when they occur *after* you have built value, created involvement, and generated some urgency to inspire the buying action. Buyers are giving you a signal when:

- *They ask more questions.* This obviously shows an interest in learning more about your product. Listen carefully, compliment them on the importance of their questions, and give more specific information on the topic to help them justify a positive decision.

- *They move closer to you physically.* In studies of proxemics (distances) experts have found that in the field of sales, when customers get close to making a purchase decision, they subconsciously but quite naturally move closer physically to the salesperson. Further encourage the physical alliance that is forming by speaking warmly. Do not change the pace of your presentation or your physical positioning at this time.

- *They move away from you physically.* When customers move away from you, they are attempting to disconnect and slow down the buying action. Lower your voice to draw them closer. Seek their feedback and input at this time, by asking a direct question that will give them an opportunity to reveal their reservations or concerns. Again, do not change the pace of your presentation; however, at the first chance possible, find a reason to move your prospect to a different location, resurface an area of agreement, and attempt to reestablish the positive proximity you had previously.

- *They clear their throat (men) or they wet their lips (women).* These signals indicate a nervousness. In sales, nervousness (the throat and mouth get dry when people get nervous) is not a negative but a positive, as it demonstrates involvement with the product and the fact that ownership is being considered. When one of these signals occurs near the point of close, it indicates a need for a breather, followed by reassurance. This is time to offer a cold drink or coffee, to change the subject for a moment and return to it with a very personalized message that offers reassurance.

- *They ask you to repeat information.* This shows an interest and determination to understand the product or service better. Sometimes the request for this information is to assist the customer in justifying his purchase to others. Give this customer a few solid facts to use as ammunition.

- *They start playing with their hair.* Both men and women make this nervous gesture when getting ready to make a purchase decision. These people need more support and reassurance that the product is what they need and that they are making a correct decision. Use phrases such as "Since you've looked around, I'm sure you will agree . . . " or "With your experience, you seem to have a good understanding of how this will help you . . . " or "Considering your situation, I feel certain this would work."

- *They start nodding their head "yes."* This rather obvious signal is often ignored by salespeople who are too involved in their own presentation to even detect this clearly visible sign of agreement. Look for this response, and progress forward with questions designed to cement the area of agreement with a verbal commitment. "So you agree that this payroll system would give your bookkeeper more time, right?" "These colors, then, would work well for you, don't you agree?"

- *They start using ownership phrases.* These little phrases, such as "I'll keep it in my desk," "We can use it to improve our newsletter," "It would look great with my taupe suit," "That would be Jenny's room," again are often disregarded by salespeople who are too busy concentrating on presenting the product to capitalize on the signals. Top salespeople are not only adept at presenting the product but are equally skilled in recognizing product reception and reinforcing it. Pause, register their involvement, repeat it in your own words for reinforcement, and move forward to a closing question.

- *They suddenly speed up the conversation pace.* Though speeding up the conversation can indicate an interest in terminating the presentation, it most often represents excitement or enthusiasm on the part of the buyer. Follow their lead, display your own enthusiasm, but do not go overboard. Stay in pace with the prospect and start positioning yourself for a close with a presentation summary.

- *They suddenly slow down the conversation pace.* Slowing down the conversation demonstrates an interest, a need for some thinking time, and a desire for some clarification. Here again, keep pace with your prospect. Display your sensitivity to their slowdown mode by leaning back in your chair slightly or by shifting to a more relaxed stance. Then demonstrate that you are willing to spend the time to clarify any point or offer more information. "Mr. Johnson, is there any more information you need on this warranty program?" "Ms. Smith, I would be glad to spend some time going into more detail about our flexible delivery schedule."

- *They change from a speaking to a listening mode.* This signal can mean a number of things. It can indicate that they are thinking things over, are still apprehensive, need more information, or are ready to buy. In any case, the customer is waiting for *you* to take the lead. First, confirm that he has all the information that he needs. Next, review what the customer just said, because most likely, his last words triggered his silence. Resolve the concern with reassurance or new information. Finally, tell her what the next step is in the buying process.

- *They raise a hand to cover their mouth in some fashion or to tug at their ear.* This usually signals the desire on the customer's part to interrupt your presentation with either a comment or concern. It is actually a modified version of the "hand-raising reflex" that we used in school to indicate that we had something to say, combined with the childhood admonishments that it is impolite to interrupt while someone else is speaking. This raising-hand-to-mouth gesture is so common in one-on-one sales that it has been labeled the *interrupt gesture.* Seeing this signal, the salesperson must stop, look at the prospect, and ask a pointed question to allow her to speak, without feeling that she has interrupted. "How does this all sound to you so far, Mr. Fulgham?" Since customer feedback is critical and customer input a necessity to sell, this signal is really one to look for.

READING A GROUP

To reiterate, reading people plays a big part in the sales process. And it is easy to see how women can use their intuition in one-on-one work with a client. But what happens if it is not one-on-one? What happens if it is ten on one and you're the one? No problem. Women even have the ability to read groups and understand group dynamics better than men. Women easily pick up on several unspoken messages simultaneously. They understand how to read patterns of communication—who talks to whom, who is in conflict with whom, who is in accord with whom, who is the leader, who is the follower, and who is the influencer.

In fact, the female brain, with almost 40 percent more connective fibers between the two hemispheres, enables women to blend the functions of conversation and observational analysis quite easily. Though women listen to words, at the same time they use heightened observation skills to notice the interaction among the group members. Women in sales, therefore, are not only able to acknowledge the signal that each member of the group sends to them, but they are also adept at registering the signals that each member of the group sends to each other. A positive group buyer signal occurs when:

- *Group members show more consideration toward each other.* Husbands and wives, bosses and secretaries, presidents and vice presidents, even board members, when making a purchase decision together, usually demonstrate more consideration and/or affection for one another right after they have nonverbally agreed that they have found the right product. As a salesperson, you must bring to the surface their unspoken message of acceptance by emphasizing that they have found a product that will meet each of their individual needs as well as the group needs. "So installing this new phone system will not only facilitate easier conference calls for the people in the shipping department, Barbara, not only enhance the intercom system for the support staff, Mark, but it will save the company as a whole considerable costs during your expansion over the next eighteen months."

There is no doubt that effective interaction with any customer requires the exchange and expression of both thoughts and feelings. Since women gain a firm handle on other people's thoughts and feelings through their intuitive powers, using these powers in the selling arena will allow them to better understand, connect with, and motivate their customers.

So intuition plays a big part in sales. But if you are uncomfortable admitting that you use your intuition to sell—just call it *sales sense,* because that's what it really is.

– 14 –
TO CLOSE FOR COMFORT
□ □ □

REASON #14
Women Know How to Wrap Up the Sale

Positioning oneself for the close is the key. Women like to recap, rehash, review, and seek agreement. Those seemingly inconsequential characteristics are the keys to open the doors for comfortably closing.

In January of 1980 I came into my office one morning to find a note from my secretary, informing me that I had been asked to speak the following week in Nashville, Tennessee, at the Grand Ole Opry Hotel, no less, for a group of saleswomen on the topic of "clothing." Though I certainly have never considered myself a fashion plate, I was well aware of the concept of dressing for success, always prided myself on looking acceptable in the business arena, stayed away from white, and always carried an extra pair of panty hose in my purse.

I was confident that with some boning up, I would most definitely be able to pull off this speech. In fact, deep down inside, I was a little flattered; maybe I really looked better than I thought. I liked this topic, "clothing," and I could even search through the catalogs, from Spiegel to Neiman-Marcus . . . to flash photos on an overhead projector of what the well-dressed woman in sales should wear. You know, I'd bring visuals.

I jotted the engagement and the topic down in my appointment book and started out that next week on a seminar circuit that would wind me up in Nashville. I realized that I had been given the last speaking slot of the daylong seminar, but

171

justified in my mind why they felt a segment on "clothing" should wrap it all up.

Well, let's face it, appearances are indeed important, and it is a pleasant topic. I mean, it was me talking to the group to give them my grooming and clothing tips, not Mr. Blackwell picking on a poor soul from the audience, criticizing her attire, and telling her that she was dressed for log rolling instead of sales. I could actually make this four-o'clock program an enjoyable and nonthreatening prelude to the cocktail hour.

I arrived at the appropriate seminar room and quietly took a seat in the back of the convention hall, prepared to enjoy the speaker conducting the half-hour segment before mine. Her topic was handling objections. She was good. I was getting a little nervous. I checked my visuals and my slip, and tried to figure out how I was going to segue smoothly from overcoming objections to clothing.

I noted the program director seated to my left and waved. She leaned over and thanked me for agreeing to speak, explaining that my topic had to be the most important of the day. I agreed, complimenting her on her unique programming format, noting that normally this topic starts a program, because we all know the cliché "You never get a second chance to make a first impression." She looked at me rather quizzically and glanced down at my Spiegel catalog. I proudly said, "Oh, I have prepared some visuals for this clothing segment." She cleared her throat, and asked if I had any dental work done lately. I now looked at her rather quizzically and asked why she said that. She responded, "Well, Nicki, you said clothing—dear, the topic, you know, is *closing!*"

My mind went berserk . . . *Closing? Closing? What? . . . Oh my God. That topic is so complex! I certainly don't have all the information memorized. Nicki, you're dead; bag the catalogs, dummy . . . It's closing, not clothing—and you'd better come up with something good and quick!*

Needless to say, the anxiety that swept through me that late afternoon in Nashville was overwhelming. But, as I immediately reminded myself, no more overwhelming than the daily anxiety of what some salespeople feel when it comes right down to closing.

Closing is the test. If you blow this step, this one step, you are done, finished, kaput. You bet there is anxiety.

When it comes down to closing, I have seen salespeople get so nervous that they can't start talking. I have seen salespeople get so excited that they can't stop talking. I have seen salespeople get so confused that they don't know what they are talking about. I have seen salespeople who have accomplished all the steps in the process that could lead to the sale, only to be riddled with frustration at not being able to close—to execute the final stage of the presentation that asks for the order.

You see, closing is the prize, the objective, the goal, the brass ring, and as such, no wonder there is a great deal of anxiety, mystery, and confusion that surrounds the topic. Entire books have been written on this subject. Weeklong seminars have been conducted on the subject. Master closers have captured the attention of vast audiences while revealing their *secrets* to closing. Supposedly there are hundreds of different closes: the either/or close, the double-question close, the alternate-of-choice close, the T-bar close, the negative-summary close, the you-deserve-this close, the I-deserve-it close, the I-need-one-more-sale-for-a-trip-to-Acapulco close, and the list goes on.

On the day of that fiasco in 1980, in attempting to come up with a new program on the spot, I found myself being forced to address the anxiety and mystery that surround closing and to streamline and simplify the process. In doing that, I was able to clarify, even for myself, the reasons for the anxiety and how to get rid of it by following just a few simple steps. But the biggest revelation of the day was in realizing that the closing formula I had come up with was tailor-made for women. I want to share that formula with you and show you how, as a woman, you can minimize the anxiety, eliminate the mystery, and close with ease.

On the surface, of all the steps in the sales process, closing doesn't seem to come quite so naturally to women. Perhaps it is because the act of closing, of asking for the order, seems to require the highest degree of assertiveness of any aspect of the sales process. That is why I want to take the mystery out of closing. I want to dispel the myth that assertiveness is the key element in closing success and reveal instead that it is positioning—setting yourself up for the sale—that creates closes. And once you see what positioning entails, you will also see why women are "closet closers"—and, ladies, it is time to come out of the closet.

Positioning for the close in the world of sales is accomplished by executing a six-step program that I refer to with the acronym "C-L-O-S-E-R." As I elaborate on the steps involved, you will see that becoming a closer luckily hinges on activities that women love to engage in. These activities are summarizing, recapping, rehashing, and reviewing.

Women love to do this. Have you noticed? How many times have you found yourself and your women friends summarizing an event, recapping a party, rehashing an incident, or reviewing a movie? It is one of women's favorite things to do. I fully expect my phone to start ringing off the hook after a shared experience with a friend so that together we can sum it all up, pull it all together, get to the essence, and agree on what occurred. And that activity, when brought into the sales process, positions you for an easy and successful close!

The C-L-O-S-E-R acronym spells out a summary process that serves to do many things. It launches the salesperson into the wind-down segment of the presentation smoothly, it gives the salesperson control, it clears up customer confusion (and a confused customer mind says "no"), it builds on logic, and it uses emotion. But bottom line—it makes it easy for the customer to say "yes."

CLOSING WITH THE C-L-O-S-E-R

Once you have presented your product and handled the objections, use a summary lead-in phrase "Mr. Jones, allow me to summarize what we talked about today . . . okay?" "Mrs. Grey, permit me to review what happened here . . .

all right?'' and then *wrap up your sales presentation with the steps that follow. You will find that they will wrap up the sale for you.*

1. Conceptualize the benefits of the product.
This requires simply highlighting the three (remember that magic number) benefits of your product that were of most importance to the prospect.
Example: "This couch has extrafirm springs, deep seating, and can be covered in a fabric of your choice.''

2. Link it to your customer's needs and/or wants.
This involves reminding her that those particular features meet the needs or wants that she has.
Example: "I know comfort as well as beauty are important to you and you will be able to match this with the other chairs in your family room.''

3. Offer your expert opinion.
This step helps the consumer to make a decision. It must be recognized that making a decision is very difficult for the average consumer. Basically, it is because people are afraid of making the wrong decision. By highlighting your expertise and knowledge of the alternatives, this step gives the prospect more confidence that buying your product is the right decision.
Example: "Based on what you are looking for, and based on what I know is available, I feel certain that you have found the perfect piece of furniture for your living room.''

4. Stress urgency.
If a prospect feels that she has time to deliberate, hesitate, think it over, and delay the buying decision, she is likely to take that course of nonaction. Your job is to use what you have learned during the conversation and tie it into a buy-now reason.
Example: "To assure that you will have delivery by Christmas.''

5. Educate the customer on the process of buying.
Almost all sales involve some sort of a purchase procedure. Educating the customer might be as simple as advising him he can pay with credit card, check, or cash. Or it could be

complex, including explaining a deposit procedure, a contract, a payment schedule, or a try and return policy, etc. Though this may sound hard to believe, when the buying process is more complex than just handing over the cash, many people don't buy because they don't know how to buy. They want to save face, not appear stupid, and therefore avoid asking how to go about making the purchase. Instead of asking any question of this type that has the chance of putting them in a subordinate position, many consumers at this point will use the "I have to think about it" response. The fact is that very often they don't have to think about it at all . . . they just don't know what to do next. The smart salesperson takes no chances; she never assumes people know how to buy . . . she tells them how to buy. And she makes it seem easy.

Example: "Let me tell you what the next simple step is."

6. **R**equest the order with confidence.

This step, of course, is the end all and be all. Oddly enough, many salespeople think that they actually ask for the order, when they really never do. They confuse step 5 with this step. In other words, they tell prospects what is needed to start the buying process rolling, but they never *ask* them to do it. There is a big difference in sales between a closing question and a closing statement. Example:

CLOSING STATEMENT:	"Ms. Johnson, if you give me a five-hundred-dollar check today, I'll be able to call the warehouse and set that shipment aside for you."
CLOSING QUESTION:	"Ms. Johnson, *can* you give me a five-hundred-dollar check today so that I can call the warehouse and set that shipment aside for you?"

Can you see the difference? Telling someone how to buy is an essential part of the process, but asking them to buy is what closing is all about! The cliché "If you don't ask, you don't get" is one you can bank on. And don't forget one other point. Once you have built rapport with the prospect and created a relationship, if you don't ask them to buy, they may think that there is something wrong with the product and you know it—that's why you are not asking them for the sale.

Now here is this concept all put together using another sales scenario:

"Mr. Jones, let's just take a moment to *summarize* what happened here today. (1) This town home has a garage, a finished family room, and two dramatic skylights. (2) I know you mentioned that you especially liked those features, and that having a finished family room was one of your top priorities. (3) Considering what you're looking for, considering what I know that is out there in the marketplace, and considering what we have here at Fox Ridge, I feel confident that you are looking at the perfect home for you and your family. (4) So you won't lose out on this wonderful opportunity, (5) let me explain how we proceed from this point (6) and then you can approve the preliminary paperwork, OK?"

Remember this CLOSER acronym. It will save your life. I don't wish to be melodramatic, but I truly believe it to be the greatest secret of closing ever revealed and the only one you really ever need to know.

My CLOSER system may seem simple, but it is powerfully effective because it enables the salesperson to easily make the transition from presenting the product to asking for the order. The funny part of it is that it all begins with what we women do naturally—summarizing—and ends with one of our other greatest gifts: seeking agreement.

15

BEING THERE

□ □ □

REASON #15
Women Send the Cards

Women, in most cases, have taken on the responsibility to follow up—to keep in touch and maintain relationships—and they are good at it. They know the importance of "being there." In sales that reaps new clients, client loyalty, and referrals.

From time to time I find myself pulling into one of those convenience stores. In the Washington, D.C., metro area we are "blessed" with 7-Elevens.

Admittedly, you have to be pretty desperate to buy anything at 7-Eleven type stores because their prices are so outrageous. For the price of a package of bologna, you could almost buy a small cow. I guess they know they are not going to sell a hell of a lot of bologna, but by charging these exorbitant prices, all they really have to do is just sell one package a week. If someone is in an emergency situation, they'll pay the price. They do and I have.

Why, then, do people *really* frequent stores like 7-Eleven? Certainly it is not for price, selection, ambience, or stimulating conversation from the checkout personnel. It's simply because at stores of this type they sell something else besides emergency supplies . . . they sell *availability*, they sell *accessibility*. And "Isn't that *convenient?*"

Their marketing strategy is based on a theory called the **Philosophy of Propinquity.**

By definition, "propinquity" refers to a **nearness.** A nearness of time, place, or relationship. The Philosophy of Propinquity espouses that **people today tend to deal with those**

who make themselves available and accessible. In other words, the convenience stores offer availability (open twenty-four hours a day) and accessibility (they are everywhere—practically at every major intersection).

The availability and accessibility factor is so attractive to today's service-denied consumers that many different types of businesses are getting on this bandwagon. Along with Domino's Pizza, pet groomers, and Federal Express, even my dry cleaner is cleaning up with this philosophy.

Understanding the busy schedules that today's lifestyles bring about, a routine dry cleaning pit stop at the local strip shopping center is not always convenient. Yet clothes need to be cleaned. Answer: a dry cleaner that picks up and delivers. And mine does just that. They make it *easy* for me to do business with them. They come to me.

Don't assume that they are particularly good at dry cleaning. In fact, sometimes I doubt that they even clean my clothes at all. I think they just put new plastic bags over them and send them back. But remember, they make it *easy* for me to do business with them; they come to me. Don't think for a moment that this service comes cheap. It costs, but remember, they make it *easy* for me to do business with them; they come to me.

If people tend to deal with people who make themselves available and accessible, then there are critical sales benefits to be gained from making it *easy* for people to do business with you. There are critical benefits to be gained from "being there," consistently and persistently.

1. **"Being there" will enable you to maintain a continuum for a sale . . . through a process called** *follow-up.*

2. **"Being there" will enable you to get new, repeat, and referral business through a process called** *awareness activation.*

FOLLOW-UP

Follow-up in sales is a key aspect of the process that separates the pros from the amateurs. Follow-up in sales works.

It enables you to move forward, get things done, and reach your goals.

Follow-up in life works, too. It enables you to move forward, get things done, and reach your goals. And who are life's follow-uppers? You got it . . . *women.*

Scenario: Two couples are ending a night of bridge. Nine times out of ten it is the woman who makes definite plans for the next get-together. "Why don't you and Rob come over to us next Sunday, OK?"

Scenario: A child promises to clean his room, brush his teeth, do his homework. Nine times out of ten, it is the mother who nags the poor kid till he gets it done. "Did you brush your teeth yet?" "What about that room?"

Scenario: You send out an invitation with an RSVP. Nine times out of ten, the response will come from a woman.

Women are naturally good at following up on a domestic level, on the home front, and with everyday occurrences. To confirm this, next time you're at the card counter, check out the ratio of men to women shoppers; next time you get those holiday greeting cards, check out the signature with the feminine script; next time you get a thank-you note, chances are it will be from a woman. The trick is now to bring this skill into the business world—and more specifically, into the sales arena.

So let's begin by heightening your awareness in terms of how follow-up works in sales, and then you will be ready to capitalize on what you already have as a woman to harness a tremendous competitive edge.

As I have said before, selling is a process. And a sale does not always occur at point of first contact with a prospect. In fact, almost all high-ticket sales (a home, boat, car, computer, trip) and even many other types of sales (radio, blender, furniture, side of beef) are not always sold on the first effort.

- Smart salespeople understand that just because your prospects do not buy the first time doesn't mean you should write them off.

- Smart salespeople recognize that making a sale often requires persistence.

- Smart salespeople realize that with high-ticket items, chances are slim that a customer will reconnect with you on their own accord.
- Smart salespeople reconnect with the potential buyer as part of the sales process and take the initiative and assertive action to arrange it.

Planning for the next contact, *establishing* the next contact, and *making* the next contact is called **follow-up.**

1.   Understand that follow-up, if exercised with a genuine interest in helping your clients buy something that will better their lives, will be viewed positively by them. It will not be seen as pushy, but instead be interpreted as caring, thoughtful, concerned, and eager.

2.   Following up during the sales process also creates value in you and your company. Image-wise, it conveys a subconscious message to the customer that you are someone who will "be there" even after the sale. And since a major customer concern today is being "dumped" after the purchase, the follow-up act in itself (if engaged in consistently and persistently) will set you and your company apart as service providers. It indicates that you will be accessible when and if your client needs you. Too many salespeople today, it seems, make the sale and then disappear into the Federal Witness Protection Program—never to be found again.

   **Remember effective follow-up requires planning. It involves setting up a reason to assure further contact and another opportunity to make a sale during each contact with the customer.

   Follow-up in sales works when you:

1.   Build a reason to follow up with the customer right into your initial meeting. If you happen to make the sale and don't have to followup to get your buyer to sign on the dotted line, all the better. But in the meantime you have provided yourself with a safety net. Your setup for follow-up may sound something like this:

"Mr. Johnson, I would like to work up some additional figures for you to show you some alternative projections. Let's meet at your convenience next week to go over them. Would Thursday afternoon or Friday morning be better?"

"I don't want to lose touch with you, Mr. Smith, because I am certain that after you mull this over, you will see that I can help you. Even if now is not the time, I would like to be able to phone you next week to give you an update on our pricing structure. Is it best if I call you in the morning on Tuesday or the afternoon?"

"Ms. Carroll, I realize you have to discuss this with your partner. However, next week I plan to be in your area, and would really appreciate the opportunity to meet with both of you. I should have the brochure of the new product line to leave with you then, as well. Can we set some time aside then for Wednesday? Is two or four o'clock better?"

2. Purposely withhold some pertinent information from the first meeting to afford you that second meeting—or feign a need to further research the answer. This step must be executed without dampening your credibility or expertise and must be done delicately. Your setup for follow-up may sound something like this:

"That is an excellent question, but I don't have all the figures with me to help you understand why we worked it up this way. If I can call you tomorrow at four-thirty P.M. with that information, I will be able to answer your question specifically."

Women seem to have an easier time using this strategy than men. Men, as we already cited, seem to be more concerned with keeping up their image as an expert or information source, and therefore have difficulty using this technique while keeping their ego intact.

3. Suggest a time to reconnect by offering your client an either/or alternative. Would two o'clock or four o'clock be better? Morning or afternoon? Weekday or weekend? This phrasing is not necessarily used to encourage the client to select one of your suggested times, but it is done to:

- Show that you are a busy and productive individual with a planned schedule

- Demonstrate your nonaggressive yet proactive leadership style

- Get your client to think in terms of specifics as well

4. Make certain that you can deliver what is promised (the callback, the mailing of additional information, etc.). The reason I broach this subject is that some people simply don't think ahead, and make promises or statements that can't be met. (I am convinced that a lot of men would call women for a *second* date if they didn't have to live up to the unrealistic expectations and exaggerations that they made on the *first* date. Do you know how hard it is to buy a Heisman trophy?)

AWARENESS ACTIVATION

The second advantage of "being there" is that it provides the opportunity to:

- generate new business
- assure repeat business
- encourage referral business

By being there, you give yourself the opportunity to first *get* them and then *keep* them thinking of you and your product or service. By being there, you activate the awareness system of your client, and that awareness cycle is hard to break.

Your job, as a salesperson of excellence, is to create in your customer or prospect an ongoing high level of awareness of you, your product, and your service. This is important so that at the appropriate times your client will naturally make the connection and think about you, become aware of you, and hopefully turn to you to do the job. Your customer must associate your name and what you are selling with any related topic, product, or opportunity.

The mind works in funny ways. Have you noticed that once something gets on your mind, things seem to happen to keep it there? Yes, in fact, we seem to see things, make "connections" and "mental associations" that reinforce what we are already thinking about.

Example #1:   When my son Billy got accepted at Tulane University in New Orleans, it seemed that as I drove around Maryland, all I saw were Louisiana license plates. I couldn't believe it. Where were they all coming from? Wasn't this strange? Of course, there was not a coincidental migration of people leaving the "Sportsmen's Paradise" and circling the Maryland beltway, it was just that I had never had reason to notice Louisiana license plates before. Louisiana was just not on my mind until Billy got into Tulane.

Example #2:   During each of my pregnancies (and in fact, once when I just thought I was pregnant), it seemed that everywhere I looked, everyone I saw was pregnant, too. I couldn't believe it. It was absolutely amazing. I never noticed before how many pregnant people were walking around. I became so aware of pregnant people that it seemed to me that practically every woman I saw was in some stage of pregnancy. In fact, I was so centered on this that I thought I even noticed a few men who seemed pregnant.

Example #3:   My husband and I were looking at some waterfront property with a broker named Philip Allahousa. When we parted company at the end of the day, my husband and I still remained undecided as to what to do. Mr. Allahousa was very accommodating and advised that if we slept on it, we would surely be back tomorrow to proceed with the purchase. While shaking hands to conclude the visit, I stumbled over his last name. He smiled and said, "Forget about my last name, just don't forget Phil. Just remember Phil." On the way home we tried to put this decision aside and talk about other things. It was almost impossible. First we passed a landfill (land "Phil") and then, when we pulled in for gas, the attendant asked if we wanted a fill-up ("Phil" up!). Continuing our drive home, I noted all the blooming "Phil"odendrons and wondered why my husband and I were considering going out for a filet ("Phil" let) mignon dinner.

What was going on here? In examples #1 and #2, the awareness system was activated to notice things that I had never paid much attention to before. This awareness was triggered by something that was on my mind. In example #3, a more complex form of awareness activation took place. I found links, suggestions, inferences, little things that seemed to trigger, reinforce, and feed my thoughts of Phil and the pending purchase—which was on my mind.

The process of activating awareness works in all aspects of life. In sales, by consciously making an effort to keep yourself in front of your clients in some way, you assure not only that they will remember you, but that they will consciously or unconsciously find reinforcement "messages" to keep the cycle going. Eventually this cycle can lead to client loyalty, new business, and referrals.

Yes, in sales this critical awareness cycle is set up by creating a sense of "being there," either in thought, spirit, or actuality. That is why little actions such as those listed below work well toward achieving this goal:

- Sending a note after a meeting
- Mailing out articles of interest
- Remembering birthdays and the like
- Acknowledging promotions or career moves
- Faxing pertinent information—or amusing anecdotes
- Providing desk pads, calendars, etc., with your name on it
- Dropping in occasionally just to say hello

These types of actions will provide you with an easy means of keeping your customer's or prospect's awareness activator system working on you. If at all possible, awareness activation methods should be creative and imaginative. Think outside the box.

Now, let's see how engaging your customer's awareness activator system can bring about:

Client Loyalty

I know one high-ticket salesperson who made it a habit to enroll each client in a fruit-of-the-month plan—expensive but it worked. Every month when the kumquats or bing cherries arrived, the accompanying note guaranteed that she was thought about—positively—and continued to be called on for business.

New Business

I also know of a super saleswoman who would stop in periodically to say hello to a potential client who swore that he was happy with his current supplier and would never change. After almost a year of spontaneous visits (sometimes with doughnuts and coffee in hand), her persistence paid off. The supplier had a slowdown in production, and the client gave his order to the saleswoman who proved that she would "be there" and wanted the business.

Referrals

Two and a half years ago, I went out and bought myself a fur coat. Now, I know this topic is one of current-day controversy, but this saleswoman assured me that the minks contributing to this particular garment all committed suicide. I accepted that.

In any event, I bought the coat and have enjoyed it immensely. I made sure this saleswoman was aware of the fact that I planned for this coat to last for years and years. I assured her that I wasn't coming back to purchase a matching hat or vest either.

An interesting thing happened, however; Mrs. Mitchell, the saleswoman, kept in touch with me. She sent me an Easter card that next spring, she sent me a Christmas card that next winter, and believe it or not, on my birthday—Steve Joy, zip; Mrs. Mitchell, a bouquet of flowers. Was Mrs. Mitchell crazy? Why would she do this? She knew this coat was going to have a home with me for a long, long time.

Mrs. Mitchell wasn't crazy, she was smart! Because though I have not visited her store once since that day two and a half years ago, I have sent three other friends to her who have purchased from her. I keep recommending her every opportunity I get. Now, if she has this deal going with twenty other past purchasers . . . she is doing great. She *is* doing great!

It isn't just flattery at work here that keeps me referring Mrs. Mitchell when I get the opportunity. It is the fact that she won't allow me to forget her. So when someone starts talking about a fur coat purchase, my mind immediately flips to Mrs. Mitchell—I can't help it. Interestingly enough, should Mrs. Mitchell start working for a competitive furrier, *she*, not her past employer, will continue to get my referrals. I know she will keep up with me to make sure that I will keep up with her too.

You will see that in sales, generating referrals is the easiest and least expensive way to do business. The client comes to you with a positive first impression and a reference from an already happy customer. The legwork and energy that you have to expend on prospecting is nil, and natural customer defenses don't exist.

Based on what effective follow-up and activating an awareness system are all about, you can easily see why women would be good at this. Most women, within their family, are in charge of sending birthday and anniversary cards, acknowledging births, weddings, and graduations, as well as responding to invitations and letters. It is usually the woman who sends out the yearly updates in Christmas card form and who is more likely to drop in on a neighbor, the elderly, a hospitalized acquaintance. Even if you have lost touch with someone over the years, it is the woman who makes the move to reestablish the connection.

Yes, "being there" in spirit or in person is a responsibility women have taken on, and we are pretty good at it. Following up and keeping the awareness system activated in business are just extensions of this.

Since many products and services aren't sold first time around, following up is a necessary part of the process. Remember, since sales today involves finding new clients, sustaining existing clients, and nurturing referrals, turning up the awareness activator system will set in motion a self-perpetuating customer base.

16

IN CONCLUSION
□ □ □

I hope this book has convinced you that as a woman, you have many of the critical abilities, skills, and tendencies that are fundamental to sell successfully to today's new breed of customers. I have also highlighted the "hows" and "whys" of many great sales techniques that you can easily incorporate into your own presentation . . . no matter what you may be selling.

Now that you know that you have the potential to be a powerful player in the world of sales, and now that you are aware of how your feminine traits have become the essence for so much of what great salespeople strive for today . . . you must take the next step. You must *do* something about it. You must make something happen. You must find a way to use these skills. The bottom line, you see, is that it is not what you know that really matters or counts . . . it is what you do with what you know that really matters.

People always ask me if there is a universal pattern among winners. I don't know about winners in other endeavors, but in the field of sales there is a definite observable force that all top producers have—they are doers. They do it. Maybe not always the right way, maybe not always the best way, but they are action-oriented people who *do*. Winners, I was told long ago, are quite simply the people who do certain things that losers just don't do. Sounds simple, doesn't it? But it has proven itself to be true over and over.

So, though you have the potential to be great in sales, having the potential is simply not enough. Potential is just the beginning. I remember reading a Peanuts comic strip in which Charlie Brown was bragging to Lucy about his incredible potential. Lucy, wide-eyed, gasped, "Wow, it must be an awesome burden walking around with all that potential."

I know that when I was a kid, supposedly I had a lot of potential, too, just like Charlie. I am not bragging about it, because I later learned that to be labeled as such was just a nice way of saying that I never did much with what I had. I remember now all those years that I wasted and am still trying to catch up. But I now understand that potential in itself means nothing . . . not in sales, not in life. It is what you do with that potential that means everything.

Though many of you may understand my premises and be inspired by the opportunities that await you, you must have the focus, energy, and persistence to go forward. I know that there are many people who feel that they must wait for the "spirit to move them" to action. Though I took physics in college and though much of it is lost to me now, I do remember one concept that one of the more esoteric teachers revealed. The spirit is lighter than the body, and the spirit will never move you, you must move the spirit.

Being a motivational speaker, I try to get people to act on their potential. I try to motivate them to take action through understanding. I try to explain to them the basic rules of motivation:

1. Everyone is motivated. Even people who are motivated to keep doing nothing are still motivated.

2. People do things for their own causes and reasons, not someone else's causes and reasons.

3. No one can really motivate anyone to do anything, because motivation is internal—it comes from something inside of you.

4. Though motivation comes from within, something heard, something read, something seen, or something felt can fan the fire and ignite the spark of your potential.

I hope that in this book I have done just that. I hope that I have not only helped you to recognize your potential and ignited that spark in some way but also given you the insight to move your spirit. And if I have done that, then you must take the next step, one that comes from within. You must get out there and make it happen.

It is difficult to make it happen with potential alone. It is difficult to make it happen unless you know what it is that you want to have happen. Setting goals helps you define what it is that you want to make happen.

GOAL SETTING

In sales, as in life, being able to establish goals, and persistently work toward those goals, is the key to success. This can be daunting to women, since we play so many roles in our day-to-day lives. Nonetheless, it is important for us to recognize that to feel complete, we must have goals within *each* one of our roles. By doing that, we will gain life direction, clarify what we are working toward, put our efforts into perspective, prioritize, and allow ourselves to ease up on a role, or to concentrate on one role over another, without guilt, for a down-the-road benefit.

I believe the most useful way to prioritize is to look at our whole lives, not just our business lives, and set goals for each aspect or role we occupy. Goals, therefore, must cover the personal, business, social, mental, physical, spiritual, and financial arenas. I have found a system that works well for me, to help prioritize my time, focus my energies, and achieve my goals. I would like to pass my secret on to you.

Begin By Talking About Your Goals

I recommend starting your goal-setting program by getting a tape recorder and recording yourself as you talk (stream-of-consciousness style) about what you want from each of the seven areas of your life. You might say a sentence or two about one area and go on at length about another area. That is no problem. I have found, since it is so much easier for most people to talk before they summarize and write, this step will allow you to hear yourself and extract from your conversation the key points.

The tape system works well, in advance of the written goal-setting procedure, because it is easily modified, can be reviewed while riding in your car or walking, and it is your own voice speaking directly to you, which adds impact to the words. Remember, what you say on these tapes does not constitute a goal. The purpose of this taping exercise is to collect your thoughts, help you discover your general wants.

I suggest you start by making seven tapes in the following categories—don't write down any goals until all seven tapes are complete, because you may have to reconsider one when considering another.

A *personal tape.* Your personal tape should contain goals for your personal life, your family plans, and your lifestyle improvements. Preparing for this tape involves thinking about your personal needs, your wants, your natural talents and abilities, the people who are going to be affected by the goals you make, and how the goals can change your life for the good. Think how much these goals are going to cost you in terms of time, money, and effort.

A *business tape.* This tape should involve plans for business development. Think about how much money you want to earn next year, five years from now. How much product or service do you have to sell to get to that point? What are you going to do to sell or service your customer better? What can you do to take business away from your competition? Who can help you achieve your goals in this area? Are there any systems that can be set up to more efficiently work toward your goals—maybe a car phone, or a fax at home, or a team approach? After you talk out your business goals, you may want to repeat some of your personal goals in terms of what benefits this money will bring to your life and to the lives of those who are important to you.

A *social tape.* Do you want to become less social or more social? Many people I know work themselves to death. On the flip side is the person who is always playing, and "Let's party" is their motto. Realistically you must assess your balance between social and work so that you can juggle effectively. Talk it out in the tape. Where do you want to go? Whom do you want to go with? How social do you want to be? How do you plan on equalizing this? What would you really like to do with your free time?

A mental tape. Think about growing mentally and expanding your mind. This is really a self-enhancement tape, because when you are done growing . . . you are done. So what is it that you are going to do to grow mentally. For me, maybe, mental enhancement includes a good deal of reading. For you, it may be taking a night course, visiting more museums, or working crossword puzzles. It doesn't necessarily have to be something highly intellectual. No matter what it is, it will help you. Remember the true sign of life is growth.

A physical tape. This tape will focus on your energy level and what you can do to enhance it. Some of us treat our bodies like we are renting. I don't believe that anyone should have an obsession with dieting, but a healthy body does just naturally have more energy. It has been said that energy is the fuel of excellence, and I have found that to be one of my personal edges in life. You can increase your energy level through proper diet, exercise, rest, and, believe it or not, through other simple measures that serve to stimulate you. Such activities as visiting with people you like or traveling somewhere different can energize you. For example, I know that whenever I call my sons, I feel invigorated. So in this tape I remind myself to do that. Your own personal experience with what gives you energy will be the basis for this tape. Define what turns you on, so you can make it happen.

A financial tape. This tape includes what you want to earn from business, but should include other things as well. Here you might also consider how to best invest the money you make, a plan to pay off loans, a timetable to start a savings plan, etc.

A spiritual tape. This tape should reaffirm some of the important principles *you* live by; what is right and what is wrong, what is good and what is bad. It means that you take the time to philosophize a little, and reevaluate your personal morals and business ethics. A tape like this gives you a chance to get in touch with your soul and puts things into perspective.

Next Start Writing Down Your Goals

Next comes a critical step. Listen to what you said on the tape during your free-flowing talk, and write down the essence of what you want to accomplish—your goals in each of the preceding areas. *Writing goals down is essential.* If your goals just stay in your thoughts or on your tape recorder, they are not goals . . . just dreams or wishes.

Now Take a Look at Some of My Guidelines for Goal Setting

1.   In order to rise to the top, you must set goals that make you stretch. But goals must be realistic, and you personally must have the power to achieve them.

2.   Limiting the number of goals is very important. Don't bite off more than you can chew. "I want to lose fifteen pounds, stop smoking, let my nails grow, stay away from red meat, and start an exercise program." Start with fewer goals, accomplish one, and add on.

3.   Goals have to be short-term. They have to be achievable within a reasonable time frame. If a goal takes too long to reach, we have a tendency to become frustrated or bored in the process of trying to accomplish it. Thirty to ninety days is the perfect time frame for a goal completion.

4.   Goals must be specific. In other words, saying you want to be the best sales producer in the company is not a specific enough goal. You must break that down to what it really requires: I want to make seven thousand dollars this month, which boils down to bringing in an additional ninety-five thousand dollars in sales.

5.   Successful goal achievement demands that you break the goal down into what specifically it is going to take to accomplish it. You cannot "do" a goal. You can only do the behaviors that will make the goal happen. You must identify the behaviors, such as bringing in more clients, targeting larger companies, concentrating more on selling upgrades wherein the profit margin is greater, aggressively pushing for referrals, etc. Also, to encourage yourself to pursue to the point of goal, you should reward yourself frequently as you accomplish some of the behaviors en route.

6. Don't be discouraged or fail to set a goal simply because you do not know how to achieve it. Realize that often we discover the behavioral objectives required *after* we set the goal. For example, in the early 1960s, when President Kennedy pronounced that by the end of the decade we would have a man on the moon, the technology did not exist for a moon landing to occur. However, once the goal was established, the route to that goal (the behavioral objectives) was developed.

7. Goals have to be re-evaluated from time to time to make sure that they are still important to you and represent what you still really want.

By starting to set goals today, you make your tomorrows work for you. Being able to discipline yourself to set goals and to do what needs to be done when it needs to be done is critical for winning, especially in a career as unstructured as sales. To be effective, you must first decide what you really want and then work toward your goals every single day.

It has often been said, "The greatest labor-saving device of today is tomorrow," and some people live by that theory. Others take it a step further and their motto becomes "Never put off until tomorrow what can be put off until the day after tomorrow." My personal philosophy is "Never put off until tomorrow what you can pull off today."

HOW TO PULL IT OFF TODAY

As a woman, you already have what it takes to become a great salesperson. And as this book has shown you, pulling it off today in sales is easier than you think. Women need only see the connection between the fifteen feminine traits I've discussed in this book and the part they play in creating a powerful winning sales approach. To make money in sales, use your:

MULTITASK ORIENTATION
INTEREST IN SEEKING OUT SIMILARITIES AND AGREEMENT
ATTENTION TO DETAIL
ABILITY TO MANIPULATE YOUR APPEARANCE AND ENVIRONMENT
WILLINGNESS TO EXTEND FLATTERY AND PRAISE
FACILITY AND COMFORT IN ASKING QUESTIONS
EXPERTISE AS AN ACTIVE LISTENER
ORGANIZATIONAL SKILLS
PROPENSITY TO TALK IN TERMS OF BENEFITS OR CONSE-
QUENCES
COMMUNICATION KNOW-HOW
INTEREST IN REACHING OUT AND INVOLVING
DESIRE FOR HARMONY AND WIN-WIN SITUATIONS
INSIGHT AND INTUITIVENESS
TENDENCY TO SUMMARIZE, REVIEW, AND REHASH
FOLLOW-UP AND FOLLOW-THROUGH

Yes, these fifteen feminine traits constitute the formula for successful selling to the new breed of today's consumer. These fifteen feminine traits provide just what it takes to gain a competitive edge. These fifteen feminine traits will work in sales . . . if you do.

Socrates said: "Once made equal to man, woman becomes his superior." I don't know if he was thinking of the sales profession when he spouted that one out, but if so . . . he really knew what he was talking about. Any woman can master the basic sales techniques and in that respect become equal to any man. But once any woman enhances those techniques with her innate fifteen feminine traits . . . she will undoubtedly be able to outsell any man.

INDEX

□ □ □